ELIMINATED!

NOW WHAT?

FINDING YOUR WAY FROM JOB-LOSS CRISIS TO CAREER RESILIENCE

Jean Baur

Eliminated! Now What?

© 2011 by Jean Baur
Published by JIST Works, an imprint of JIST Publishing
7321 Shadeland Station, Suite 200
Indianapolis, IN 46256
Phone: 800-648-JIST   Fax: 877-454-7839   E-mail: info@jist.com

Visit our Web site at **www.jist.com** for information on JIST, free job search tips, tables of contents, sample pages, and ordering instructions for our many products!

Quantity discounts are available for JIST books. Please call our Sales Department at 800-648-5478 for a free catalog and more information.

Trade Product Manager: Lori Cates Hand
Interior and Cover Designer: Toi Davis
Proofreaders: Laura Bowman, Jeanne Clark
Indexer: Jeanne Clark

Printed in the United States of America
15 14 13 12 11 10   9 8 7 6 5 4 3 2 1

Library of Congress Cataloging-in-Publication Data

Baur, Jean, 1946-
  Eliminated! Now what? : finding your way from job-loss crisis to career resilience / Jean Baur.
     p. cm.
  Includes index.
  ISBN 978-1-59357-816-9 (alk. paper)
  1. Unemployment--Psychological aspects. 2. Job hunting. 3. Career changes. I. Title.
  HD5708.B38 2011
  650.14--dc22
                                    2010031609

ISBN 978-1-59357-816-9

CONTENTS

Part 3: Turning the Corner, or The Way Forward 141

Appendixes

Dedication

For my father, John Ireland Howe Baur, who always believed,
and for my mother, Louisa Chase Baur, who shared a deep love of writing.

Acknowledgments

Special thanks to my neighbor Neal Rist, who introduced me to career counseling and the outplacement industry. For Orville Pierson, my colleague at Lee Hecht Harrison, whose passion for marketing helped me put together a winning book proposal, and whose enthusiasm kept me going at low moments. I'm deeply grateful for the incredible experience of having my work in the hands of an excellent editor, Lori Cates Hand, who made the process fun. For all the clients I've had the pleasure to work with over the past 16 years, I deeply appreciate being part of your transitions. And lastly, a big hug to Henry, who started it all.

INTRODUCTION

WORKING TOWARD CAREER RESILIENCE

I was recently asked to write a book about recession-proof careers, and when I thought about it, I realized that I didn't believe in the concept. Sure there are occupations like nursing or teaching that are probably mostly recession-proof, but what I see in my role as a career counselor who has worked with thousands of people in transition over the past 16 years, is that there are *people* who are recession-proof. These are the ones who know how to get up off the floor when they're knocked down by job loss and run a good search. They're creative about their goals and their methods of reaching them. They're resilient.

This book is about job loss and how to get through it effectively. The examples and case studies expose you to what others have done, showing what has led to a successful search as well as behaviors that have caused problems. Reading about others in this process solves a critical issue that most people experience in losing a job and looking for a new one: isolation. It's a shock to many of my clients to learn that others going through this also can't sleep, feel lost, aren't managing their time, don't know what to do, are irritated by their families, and have a hard time believing that they'll ever work again. As a senior IT client said to me after a month of looking for work, "I'm in purgatory."

In my own career, I've been downsized and have also had to make radical occupational changes. In fact, I fell into my current position as a career counselor in the outplacement industry through a strange series of events. Sixteen years ago I had completed a five-year assignment as a freelance writer for a local educational company. I wasn't formally downsized, but the work dried up, so I was no longer needed. I realized that although I was good at the work (my nickname was "Jean the writing machine"), I didn't particularly want to do it any longer.

Prior to that job I had worked extensively as a corporate trainer, flying all over the country to deliver seminars on business writing and presentation skills. I was good at that too, but burned out, becoming tired of teaching the same classes and really tired of the travel, especially with a young child at home. So there I was with two professions under my belt and no clear direction. No way forward. And I needed to work—both financially and emotionally. In addition to paying my bills, I wanted to feel useful and connected to other people, not limited to conversations with my family and the cat and dog.

This was 1994 and the war in Bosnia was at its height. I realized only much later that Peter Jennings, then the anchor of ABC's nightly news, influenced me. He took a personal interest in the war, traveling to Bosnia, interviewing adults and children, and exposing viewers to the horrors that seemed to escalate by the day. As I watched images of bullet-pocked homes and markets being blown up, and read of the shortages and hardships the people there were facing, I decided I had to do something.

I will share this story in detail later in the book, but the point for now is that this effort of organizing a committee through my church, and eventually sponsoring a refugee family of five, helped me realize other things that I'm good at. It brought me out of myself, put my job search in perspective, and gave me confidence, so that when a neighbor suggested that I might want to look into the outplacement industry, I was ready to say "yes."

As I tell my clients, recovering from job loss and looking for a new opportunity is rarely a straight line. And in some cases, it's a wild trip. So fasten your seatbelts, and let's explore what you may be experiencing and how others have worked through it, in this season of tremendous challenge in our economy where the lingering effects of layoffs, downsizings, and plant closings are dominating our lives. And my hope is that by learning what others have done when confronted with job loss, you'll join the ranks of the resilient and recession-proof workforce.

A Note on Confidentiality: None of the examples in this book are based on a single client. What I've done is to stick to things that really happened, but to draw from several resources to both make a point and to protect my clients' anonymity. In the outplacement field, as in other kinds of counseling, confidentiality is critical. Information from one client doesn't go to another or to colleagues. But at the end of each part, I've included a chapter in a client's own words, so that in addition to hearing from me, you'll also get the perspective of a person who has recently experienced job loss.

Most importantly, I want to thank all of the clients who have allowed me to be part of their transitions. They are the ones who have taught me how to succeed in a challenging and critical process.

PART 1

IT CAN'T BE
HAPPENING TO ME

CHAPTER 1

THE SHOCK

There are almost always signs before you lose your job, but many times you don't see them until after the fact. So you're called into a meeting with your boss, and someone from HR is sitting there as well, and they both look as if they'd like to sink through the floor. You are politely told to have a seat. And as you wonder why you're there, you're told that, due to

- restructuring,
- downsizing,
- acquisition,
- loss of business, or
- the current financial crisis,

you're no longer needed. And then they might reassure you that this has nothing to do with your performance, in fact... (this is the point where you can't hear anymore and you're sure this is a bad dream or hallucination). So their mouths keep moving but nothing is sinking in. And if the company has thought this through carefully, someone like me, a career counselor from an outplacement firm, is waiting in the next room to talk to you.

You are ushered in and told that here is a resource that your company is providing for you. And then you sit down with a complete stranger and want to cry. And this sympathetic man or woman is talking but it's impossible to pay attention, so you nod, are given a packet of information, and then are escorted to the HR office where you endure another lecture—this time about your benefits.

Depending on your company's style and industry, you might be allowed to go back to your desk to get your things. Or you might be escorted out of the building by an armed guard after handing over your badge and any other company property. You may have to arrange to go back another day, after hours, to get your personal effects. So here you are on the sidewalk or in the parking lot, and in the course of less than an hour your whole world has been turned upside down.

It's strange to be out of the building at this time of day. You look around and people are busily going places. Somehow you get yourself home. You call your spouse or best friend. You tell them you were let go. Anger and fear compete for the top emotion. Disbelief is close behind. Someone somewhere made a mistake. They can't do this. The department needs you. You're the only one who knows how to…. And now you're thinking about the hard work you did on your most recent project and part of you hopes that it will grind to a halt without you.

But the phone doesn't ring and you have a packet of papers with you that proves this is not a reversible decision. And then you think about the signs—the meeting you weren't invited to, the way your boss dodged the bonus chat, the closed doors, the gossip—and you kick yourself for not being prepared. Why didn't you see this coming? What should you do now?

KEEP THINGS SIMPLE

What you do in the first few days of job loss matters. So first of all, recognize that this is an emotional time, a difficult transition, and that you're not making any big decisions. Secondly, you want to keep your dignity intact. You don't want to lash out at your boss or former boss and coworkers. If you've been let go, you need simply to get out of the office and go home.

Call your spouse or best friend, get back to your home, make yourself a nice lunch, and then take a walk or do something that allows you to burn off some of the hurt and anger. It's too soon to update your resume or begin calling your contacts. Keep things simple.

When I met with Jim he was stunned. It was the end of the work day and he had been called into his boss's office and told that his job had been eliminated. He was a Project Manager at a major pharmaceutical firm and had been with the company for 10 years. His work had gone well and he was regularly promoted. After he was ushered into the room where I was waiting for him, he politely shook my hand and then said, "I shouldn't be here."

"I'm sorry to meet you under these circumstances," I replied.

"You don't get it. My work is critical."

He looked down at the floor and I waited to see whether he was going to say anything else. After an awkward silence, I said, "It's very hard to understand these business decisions, but in my work, I see this all the time. That is, I meet with people who are really good at what they do but that doesn't mean they won't be downsized."

"Why would they do this?" he asked me.

"I don't know the answer to that, but I'm here to let you know about the services you have with my company that will help you move forward."

"I just can't believe it," said Jim, a bit more softly this time.

I then asked him to tell me about his work and what he was particularly good at.

We also discussed the job market and how he might use his outplacement services. I found out which of our offices was most convenient for him and signed him up for a seminar that would get him started. In the course of our conversation, he told me that he lived in New York City but worked in New Jersey and usually got a ride to the train station with a coworker. So we asked HR to hire a car to drive him back to his apartment in the city. We could have asked for a ride to the train station, but he and I agreed that, given the circumstances, it was the least the company could do for him. He told me later that riding in that hired car gave him the quiet and private time to begin processing his job loss and what he might do next.

Quick Do's and Don'ts

Do:

1. Get yourself home and call your most supportive friend, relative, or spouse.

2. Have a cup of tea or coffee and make yourself lunch or a snack.

3. Take a walk or do something that involves physical effort, such as cleaning, sorting through a closet, raking leaves, or grooming the dog.

4. Make a list of the things you may need to do, but don't do them yet.

Don't:

1. Start calling your network.

2. Make frantic calls back to your now-former coworkers.

3. Repeat over and over how awful your company is—this will only make you feel worse.

4. Second-guess why you were let go. In most cases you won't know the reasons. Deciding what they are when you're upset adds insult to injury.

Resources and Ideas

Sometimes these suggestions aren't enough. After a day or so you may find yourself in a funk: not getting out of bed, not taking care of yourself, and feeling despondent. How people get out of this very difficult place seems to vary widely. Here are some of the resources that the clients I've worked with have found helpful:

- **Therapy:** You're entitled to four free sessions through your company's Employee Assistance Program (EAP) under the Employee Assistance Act. Call the confidential number posted on your former company's Web site to set up an appointment with a therapist. This is kept 100 percent confidential, so no one else at your former company will know that you're using this resource. If after the four sessions the therapist thinks you need to continue, you can then be referred to someone else. If your insurance doesn't cover this, make sure to tell the therapist that you're in transition (that's the cheerful way to say you're out of work). Some charge on a sliding scale.

- **Physical exercise:** One client from several years ago had gone through a terrible trauma. Her four-year-old son had died about a year before she lost her job. Job loss was easy compared to that. After she and I got to know each other, I asked her how she got through that very difficult time, and she told me that going to the gym every day and working out helped her sweat and grunt through the pain. It didn't take it away, but it gave her one part of her life that was under her control and it exposed her to other people—her trainer and the others at the gym. And because the training was demanding, it didn't allow her to think about her son the whole time.

- **Volunteering:** By helping others, whether they're people being fed at a soup kitchen, children with special needs, or animals at a shelter, your situation may look less grim. Volunteering can give you perspective, make you feel useful, and again, put you in contact with others. Another benefit is that those who volunteer often find that the strangers they meet through this activity want to help them.

CHAPTER 2

GIVE UP ASKING "WHY?"

So if you're in the first mind-numbing days of job loss, you may find yourself going round and round like a gerbil on an exercise wheel. You were dedicated, went the extra mile, stayed late, and loved your job—none of this makes sense. This can feel like having a loose tooth—you keep fussing with it and that only makes it hurt more. The "what-ifs" invade your brain so that every other minute you're asking yourself, "What if I had offered to stay late for that meeting?" or "What if I hadn't had that argument with my boss?" or "What if they hadn't hired that new guy who made me look bad?" And so on.

I tell my clients that this is where they need to build the Great Wall of China—or a moat filled with sharks.

You cannot go there because it's unproductive and hurtful. Try to get yourself to face forward rather than backward and set up good, strong habits that will sustain your job search and get you away from the "why" question. These could include

- Getting up each day at the same time as you did for work
- Setting a job search schedule for yourself (see appendix A for examples)
- Educating your family or support system about what you need and what you don't need
- Using outside resources, which might include an outplacement program; taking classes on interviewing, networking, or writing a strong resume through the local unemployment office; or attending local job search support groups
- Having a search buddy you check in with daily to stay accountable
- Getting regular exercise
- Volunteering

This is also a time to be nice to yourself. If you've always wanted to learn how to paint, find a local class, get the supplies, and give yourself that gift. If massage helps you relax and feel pampered, barter for a massage or find a place that offers reasonable rates. If you can't stand the color of your bedroom, get the paint and maybe some outside help, and transform it into a place you really enjoy. A woman on a team that I facilitate decided to dye her hair a new color as a way to get out of her fear and anxiety. This was her gift to herself and also reminded her, every time she looked in the mirror, that she was becoming a new person. And it also looked really nice.

What's the magic of these tasks? How do they help? I don't know the full answer except to say that action is better than inaction. Getting something done breeds satisfaction. Mindless tasks such as cleaning out a closet or recycling your old paint cans makes space for something new. My advice is try them, cling to them; because without your really knowing why, they begin your recovery.

TAKE SMALL STEPS

Okay, so mindless tasks are a great place to begin. Action is better than inaction. Getting out of bed beats not getting up. Find something that can give you a little satisfaction. Cleaning the house or building things seems to work for many people. But be creative about it. If you've always wanted to take tap-dancing lessons and never had the time, find a class, sign up, and buy the shoes. Coaching a sport or becoming a mentor are other ways to go. Not only will these tasks begin your recovery, but they'll also be good for your network. They'll get you energized and connected with others.

And it's okay if you're not ready for this yet—if the question "why?" is still weighing heavily on you and you can't stop asking it. If even simple actions are more than you can handle, just pay attention and look for little ways to begin. Remind yourself that in most cases you won't know the reason why you were let go, and others won't perceive this as unusual or as having anything to do with who you are or your performance at work.

A lawyer I recently worked with loved golf and got involved with an organization that uses teaching at-risk children how to play golf as a way to share important values. She had been involved with this group before she was let go, but once her free time expanded, she found great comfort in doing more with them. I see this as the perfect reward: You work on your resume, make a few difficult calls, research your top companies, and then, when you've made a good effort for the day, you can leave all that behind and do something else.

Quick Do's and Don'ts

Do:

1. Recognize your strengths, what you're good at, and what you enjoy doing. Those haven't changed. *Only* (and it's a huge "only") your employment status has. So your experience, education, skills, and attributes are all exactly the same as they were before. Tell yourself this many times every day.

2. Schedule something that you can look forward to. This could be a movie date, lunch with a friend, or a walk in the park. Try to put several of these enjoyable events on your calendar every week.

3. Begin making a list of your work accomplishments—where you made a difference. It doesn't matter what role you played—as an administrative assistant or as the CFO—you need to write down some specific examples of the ways you improved efficiency, created a new process, or whatever.

4. Think about what you liked and didn't like about your past job. It's important to use this time, this involuntary break from work, to do some career planning. Most of us fall into jobs, hang onto them for dear life even if we hate them, and never take the time to evaluate or plan what we really want to do. Of course this has to be balanced with your finances, but even if you need another position quickly, it's good to go after the jobs that will be rewarding.

Don't:

1. Keep asking "why?" and getting into long conversations with the people you used to work with. This leads nowhere and will not make you feel better.

2. Assume you were let go because of something you did or didn't do. Don't confuse performance with what I call "financial musical chairs."

3. Take it personally. I have to tell you this is a really hard one for me as I take everything personally, even the weather. So try a little mantra, such as "This has nothing to do with me," and repeat it as often as you can.

4. Assume there's a stigma to being out of work. When I started working as a career counselor in 1994, there was still a bit of a question about why someone was let go. Now, with the huge numbers we're seeing all over the country, it's a non-event. No one thinks anything of it; and in fact, as you talk to people, you'll find that it's getting increasingly difficult to find someone who hasn't lost a job at least once.

Resources and Ideas

Again, this is a very personal part of the process of getting yourself turned around facing the present and the future. Some people find help from motivational reading or audio resources. Others use prayer as a way to get unstuck. Exercise can be liberating for still others. Research may work for someone else—looking into new career paths, finding out the requirements, taking classes and getting certifications, and so on.

- One of the keys to getting beyond the *why* question is hope, which is often best articulated in works of literature. For example, my favorite Emily Dickinson poem is this:

  "Hope" is the thing with feathers—
  That perches in the soul—
  And sings the tune without the words—
  And never stops—at all—

And sweetest—in the Gale—is heard—
And sore must be the storm—
That could abash the little Bird
That kept so many warm—

I've heard it in the chillest land—
And on the strangest Sea—
Yet, never in Extremity,
It asked a crumb—of Me.

- A book that I've found tremendously helpful over a number of years is *The Artist's Way: A Spiritual Path to Higher Creativity* by Julia Cameron. What's neat about this book is that the author believes that we're all creative and meant to be creative, although this can take many different forms. The book offers a step-by-step approach to recognizing and nurturing your own creativity and is filled with a wide range of exercises and examples that can help you get to know yourself on a deeper level. I believe this can be very useful for rebuilding your self-esteem and confidence and for helping you explore work that taps into your creative interests.

- Think of someone whose advice you'd appreciate and ask them to talk with you for a half-hour. Face-to-face is always better than on the phone (if practical) because most people are more generous when you're in front of them. Prepare for this meeting with a list of questions, but don't be surprised if the agenda shifts. If this person is paying attention to your needs, they may have ideas that are new to you. Do your best to stay open and consider them.

- Talk to your family doctor, rabbi, minister, priest, or other spiritual advisor so that they know what you're going through and can offer their perspective. These conversations are confidential, and many people feel a bit better knowing someone else has heard them and is supporting them. As you'll see in the next chapter, hiding what has happened to you almost always makes things worse.

CHAPTER 3

DON'T HIDE UNDER A ROCK

This one is a bit embarrassing and you may not want to admit that you've shared any of these thoughts. That's okay. I'm including this story because if it sounds a bit familiar, you'll know you're not the first one to feel this way.

Here's the example. A man loses his job. We'll call him Bill. Bill is a manager at a large company and has been there for 15 years. He's good at his job and likes it. He's comfortable. He knows everyone in his department and lots of others as well. He's promoted regularly. His life is in order and it's predictable. He parks in the same space every morning at the same time. He says the same thing to the receptionist on his way to his office. He puts his coat on a hanger on the inside of his door. He checks his e-mail, looks at his calendar for the day, prioritizes his work, and gets it done. He eats lunch with the same group of friends in the company cafeteria at the same time every day. Okay, you get the picture.

Then one day Bill is called into his boss's office and gets the dreaded message that he's laid off. Bill gets himself home and calls his wife, who works part-time. He tells her not to tell the children. She agrees. So Bill takes off to the local library and stays there until the time he always left work, and then he drives home. His children are fighting over whose turn it is to pick the TV program, and they don't look up as he walks into the room. He says hello to them in the same way he has every other day and goes upstairs to change.

His wife, who is in the middle of making dinner, comes upstairs with him and gives him a big hug.

"I'm so sorry," she says. "I really can't believe it."

Bill thanks her and changes his clothes and the topic of conversation.

"What's for dinner?" he asks, sounding like one of the kids.

His wife stands there, speechless.

"Are you alright?" she asks.

"Yup. Should have seen this one coming, but I'm fine. Several others were let go today, too."

"But—"

Before his wife can say anything more, Bill walks out of the room and downstairs. At dinner the talk doesn't vary from any other evening at their home. Afterward, he tells the kids to get their homework done, watches a few shows on TV, reads the paper, and goes to bed.

The next day, he gets up at his usual time, 6:30 a.m., takes a shower, gets dressed in a suit, and eats breakfast with the family. He chats about a project he's working on. His wife sits there, unable to eat. He takes his dishes to the kitchen, kisses everyone goodbye, and heads out "to work." Only today he has no place to go and the library isn't open yet.

He finds a coffee shop, checks out some job boards on his laptop, and then spends the rest of the day at the library. This elaborate ruse is not only fooling his children—all his neighbors and friends (except the ones from his company) are clueless. They think his life is unchanged. They have no reason to offer help because they believe he's still working. And his plan is to keep doing this until he has a new job, and then he'll share the information with others if he feels like it.

So, what's wrong with the picture? Why not pretend that everything is just as it was? Isn't it better to protect young children? First of all, sustaining this pretense takes a lot of energy—energy you need for your search. Secondly, you are virtually guaranteeing that you will have almost no help from your network because no one knows you're looking for work. And lastly, this ruse ties you to the past—to your past job, past schedule, and so on, and therefore makes it much harder to move forward.

Of course, families need to make the best decision as to what they tell their children. A two-year-old probably won't get it. But what I see quite often in my work is that job seekers with young children often find this a special opportunity because they get to spend more time with them. And of course this can't happen if you're pretending to be at work.

Pride gets in the way of telling neighbors, and again, this is a personal issue. There may be neighbors you'd prefer not to share this information with and that's fine. But as you organize your networking list, and as you think about the people you know from your most recent position, past jobs, your community, family, and so on, you'll decide how you want to start reaching out to people.

There are often two different schools of thought on this one: It's easier to start with the people you know, or it's easier to start with people you're referred to but don't know well. I don't think it matters as long as you find a way, when you're well prepared, to share the information that will help others help you.

CREATE AN EFFECTIVE NETWORK

Here's an example that is the antithesis of Bill. A client on my job seekers' team (this is a weekly meeting that helps our clients in transition get and stay productive) was in his fifth month of searching. Severance was running out and he couldn't support himself and his family on unemployment benefits. He organized his networking list into categories: people who knew him very well and who he could be sure would help him, those he knew less well but who had strong connections, and "stretch" contacts—people whom he might be able to reach through referrals. He set a quota for the week so that this critical reaching out to people couldn't slip through the cracks. Some he contacted by e-mail; others he called. He kept a spreadsheet so that he knew when he contacted them, what they discussed, and when he'd follow up, as well as who had his resume or his list of top companies. He was systematic and organized but also flexible. Sometimes the conversations veered off into unexpected topics. He knew that was okay and often might lead to additional help or advice. And if he was having a bad day, he might skip this effort, but he kept to his quota by making it up the next day.

And because he had to pay attention to the very real financial pressures he was facing, he explored contract work and what I call some "plan B" options. These were positions that might not have been exactly what he wanted, but might be easier to get. They could be temporary, could involve lower-level positions, or could even be farther from home.

So the difference here is that Bill was off by himself and couldn't access the resources that others might add to his search, whereas the client on my team was a public relations machine. And besides the obvious differences, the client who was reaching out felt better because he was connected to others and was supported by them, and his world was expanding.

Quick Do's and Don'ts

Do:

1. Prepare a simple, clean message about why you were let go. These statements are often built around reorganizations, acquisitions, loss of sales, a reduction in force, outsourcing, and so on. Test it on a few people to make sure there are no red flags.

2. Start creating a list of the people you know. List making is a magical activity in my opinion because the process of doing it almost always helps you think of others. Many job seekers I've partnered with, after a week or two of working on this list, think of a really wonderful contact who can open doors for them.

3. Be aware that this is a tricky time for most people going through it and move slowly. You want a strong foundation before you jump into networking and interviews.

4. See if there is one small action you can take today that will help you move forward. This could be reading through your resume, making a list of your key strengths, or thinking about the work you've enjoyed the most.

Don't:

1. Hide, but rather find your own pace and style, and when you're ready, begin sharing your news with others.

2. Let your bitterness or anger come through in your conversations except with your closest friends.

3. Introduce yourself in the past tense, such as "I used to be an IT Manager." It's much better to say, "I am an IT Manager, most recently with XYZ Company and I'm excited to be looking for...." (By the way, this is one of the few times that I think it's just fine to lie. You may not be one bit excited, but say it anyway because eventually your emotions will catch up with your words.)

Resources and Ideas

As you begin to feel a bit less in shock and are adjusting to your new situation, you might be ready to read a book or two or to attend a class that will help you. The class might not be about job loss or how to job hunt effectively, but it could be something that adds to or updates your skill set. For example, I'm working with a marketing client who is learning how to use Dreamweaver so that she can enhance her Web design skills.

- Go to the library and take out a few books on job hunting skills and career assessment. If you need suggestions, take a look in the "Suggested Reading" section in appendix H.

- Ask others who are in this process or who have gone through it recently what helped them.

- Think of people you admire and make a list of what it is about them that makes them special.

- Find activities that give you perspective. One client told me recently that he tries to view his job search as "a speed bump in his life." In other words, it's a bit rough right now, but things will change. These activities can be quite different. Some gain perspective from a retail job, others from consulting or contract work, and still others by helping others. Finding a job lead for someone else in transition not only makes you feel better, but it also motivates the recipient to help you in return.

- Look for quotations or cartoons that make you smile. I love the *New Yorker* job search cartoons and often post them in the office. My recent favorite shows a hiring manager behind a desk that is made entirely of rejected resumes.

CHAPTER 4

BE PREPARED FOR THE UNEXPECTED

If looking for a new job were predictable, if someone like me who is a career counselor could say to you, "Look, I know this is a difficult process, but in three months you're going to land a terrific job," you'd say to yourself, "Okay, this isn't so bad. I can do it." But no one can tell you this because no one knows either the length of your job search or the specific outcome.

There are formulas out there that claim "for every $10K you earned, add a month to your search," and other generalizations that the higher your level, the longer your search will take. What I tell my clients is that if anyone says how long your search will take, run out of the room. Get out fast because they don't know what they're talking about.

As a very clever client of mine once said, "Hope for short, prepare for long." So what does this mean? First of all, I think it means to commit to the process. You're in a process that requires effort and hard work, and often you won't see the results right away. Secondly, create a strong foundation. Get your verbal communications (about your goals, why you were let go, your key accomplishments, and so on) in order, prepare your resume and get feedback on it from a number of sources, and make a map (this is really just a bunch of lists) to show your key strengths, the industries you'd like to work in, and most importantly some companies you plan on investigating. (See appendix C for examples.)

But no matter how carefully you plan and prepare, weird things happen. For example, your best friend from your most recent job doesn't call you back. Your boss, who swore that he or she was happy to be a reference, won't answer your e-mails. Someone else whom you've networked with in the past falls off the planet. But this is only half of it. As you struggle to move ahead (and all experts agree that networking is key to a productive search), you tentatively reach out to some people you don't know. Maybe they're experts in your field or they work for a company that's of interest to you. And without warning a huge door opens and they invite you in. They want to talk with you, connect you to others, and share information. They act as if they're glad to hear from you. How strange is that?

I can see in my clients' eyes, when I tell them this, that they think I'm crazy. Off the deep end. Up until now, they've tolerated me, even though they never leave my office without homework. But now they're thinking: *I'll nod, I'll agree to whatever Jean is saying, and then I'll never come back.*

Why is this so threatening? There are people out there who want to help you, maybe because you're referred by someone they know and like, maybe because it feels good to help others, or perhaps out of curiosity and wanting to build their own network. Here's a really interesting thing: As you get into your job search, you begin to know what it's like "out there." This means you know something about the job market, the hiring process, working with recruiters, interviewing, and so on. This is invaluable information. It's gold. Why? Because the people who are still working, unless they're totally oblivious, know that it might not be very long before they too are "out there." And even if by some miracle their jobs are secure, market information is always useful because it keeps us current and may help a company improve its strategy or services.

If this cheerful news sounds really odd to you and you're not ready to believe it, that's okay. Just don't assume that you know what's going to happen. Don't decide that what is going on now (which is usually not much at the beginning of a job search campaign) is a prediction of things to come. It's not. This is a process that requires preparation, practice, patience, and perseverance. And don't forget courage. So one small effort at a time, one obstacle at a time, you'll work through it and make progress. But you have to be willing to begin.

MANAGE YOUR EXPECTATIONS

Here's a story from a client on my team. He was running a textbook search. He was doing everything right. He used Internet resources but wasn't addicted to them; he learned how to network; he attended professional association meetings; and he used a proactive approach—using his list of companies to get others to help him. And although his search wasn't dead, not much was happening.

After several months of this, his face started to sag. He was generous and helped others, and was clearly happy when other clients on the team landed new jobs. But one day, as he was leaving the room after the team meeting, he said to me, "Will I ever land? I don't know what else to do."

This was a hard question, and as I thought about it, I honestly couldn't think of any ways he needed to revise his search. On my way home that evening, I thought about "luck," which is a concept we don't usually talk about in the outplacement world. But there is something to being at the right place at the right time, and I do think some of that can be attributed to luck or chance.

We made his question an agenda item at the next job seekers' team meeting. He got input from others, and like "The Little Engine That Could," he continued putting in the hours and the effort to find a new job. One day, not long after this, his teenage daughter asked him if she could give his resume to the father of one of her friends. He wanted to say, "Go ahead, give it to the whole world if you want.

It won't make any difference," but instead he told her it was fine and that he appreciated her thinking of him.

Two days after that his phone rang. This man, the father of his daughter's friend, was in a senior position at a small but growing company in the area, and they needed a new person in operations—his area of expertise. When I walked into the conference room the following Monday for our weekly team meeting, he was sitting in his usual place, a huge grin on his face, with a box of donuts in front of him.

"No!" I said, so excited that I was nearly speechless.

"Oh, yeah," he answered, bursting with relief and happiness.

Because I knew he'd go through the whole story with the team, I waited until our meeting started, and then learned how his daughter helped him get the connection that led to this offer. Not only was this a perfect fit for him, but also the whole hiring process was lightning-fast. He went from phone conversation to an interview to an offer in less than a week. He had two glorious weeks ahead of him with nothing to worry about and then would start his new job.

In his final report to the team, he shared what he had learned: Keep going, look for help from unexpected places, be generous to others, follow leads that may seem doubtful, assess how you're doing on a regular basis, and refine your goals and methods of searching as you go.

So the unexpected in his case was help from his daughter. Because the search process can be difficult and frustrating, it's easy to feel that the "unexpected" will only bring more bad news. I like to tell my clients to prepare for luck—to make it easier for luck to find them, by doing exactly what this client did: Work the process, keep at it, and be open to chance and new ideas.

Quick Do's and Don'ts

Do:

1. Try your best to keep an open mind. At the very least, admit that you don't know what will happen.

2. Ask for help. This is a tough one for many of us because we perceive this as a weakness. Look for small ways to begin.

3. Get your finances in order. Sit down with a financial planner or a friend who's a CPA and see how long your severance and unemployment will last. Make a budget and look for ways to reduce your expenses. The IT job seeker I mentioned in the introduction wouldn't let his family turn on the air-conditioning during the summer except on the hottest days because he was so concerned about saving money. Many clients give up going out to dinner and cut back on other extras. If you want to really cut way back, the *AARP Bulletin* recently ran an article about the "simplicity movement"—families and communes that have found ways to live creatively on radically reduced budgets.

4. Begin work on your resume. Those of us in the outplacement industry recognize that resumes by themselves don't get jobs. But still, a strong, clear one that sells your strengths is critical.

Don't:

1. Watch the news. Okay, if you have to, watch a little news, but not all day. Limit yourself to not more than half an hour a day; otherwise your head will be filled with statistics about how bad the economy is and how another million workers just lost their jobs. This is toxic and you can only take small doses.

2. Ask for sympathy. This never works, and it undercuts your strong message about yourself: that you have something important to offer. Okay, ask your best friend for five minutes of sympathy a day, but that's it. Again, small doses.

3. Assume you know how long your search will take. You don't; I don't; no one does. This is a process that is filled with unpredictability, and when you're feeling discouraged you can think you know that it will take months and months. But you don't.

4. Believe that where you are today—in terms of how you're feeling and how your job search is going—is where you'll be tomorrow or the next day. This is similar to number 3, but has to do with not understanding the volatile nature of this endeavor. I've had clients put in months of hard work, come into my office in despair, and then a day or two later call to tell me that they now have interviews at two different companies. Things can change very quickly and often do.

Resources and Ideas

As mentioned earlier, I often say to my clients, as we get to know each other and they hopefully are beginning to trust me, "Fasten your seatbelts," meaning that turbulence is part of the process. Rejection is inherent. We may never like it and it may always sting, but to think that every interview will result in an offer is to have unrealistic expectations.

And a career coach or a well-meaning friend can tell you that not getting the job isn't personal. But when it's you selling yourself, you trying so hard to fit in and convince the interviewers that you really can be a productive part of this team, and then they either never get back to you or weeks later let you know that they've decided to hire someone else, it's painful. It reopens the initial wound of job loss. It brings you down. So what can you do to prepare yourself for rejection?

- Duke Ellington once said, "I merely took the energy it takes to pout and wrote some blues," which means to me you experience the disappointment, you acknowledge it, and then you do your best to turn it into something else so that it doesn't paralyze you.

- A senior procurement client landed a wonderful new job after running a proactive and creative search, and he told colleagues from his former company, when they were let go a few months after his departure, "Use your time positively to get yourself established. Don't look back."

  (Another interesting thing about him: He had a business on the side that his wife helped him run, and the job that he ultimately accepted was a rough commute—about 80 miles each way on congested highways. He used the side business to feel productive at low moments in his search and didn't allow the commute to stop him from accepting a wonderful job with a strong company. He adjusted to the commute and made it work. And when I talked with him a few weeks ago, he told me that he had already been promoted.)

- Hope for short, prepare for long. It's a little easier to process rejection if you haven't set up unrealistic deadlines for your search.

- Keep your pipeline full. If you're pursuing only one job lead and things look great, but then it falls through, you're left with no activity, no leads, and very little encouragement. By running a diverse and healthy search—meaning you're using various methods to generate activity and you're going after a number of companies—you'll always have something to fall back on.

- Remember that there are many variables that determine who gets hired, and you may not know all of them. So when you're turned down and don't get an offer, see what you can learn from the experience, but also remind yourself that you did a really good job and that you're getting closer to an offer.

CHAPTER 5

RECLAIM YOUR VALUE

Here's a really surprising thing: People who were the most dedicated, who went the extra mile at work, who stayed late, and who saved critical projects often have the most difficulty adjusting to being laid off. I think this is because they believe (and it's a reasonable expectation) that they're indispensable and that they've earned a kind of protection through their excellent performance. Wrong.

The "who gets laid off and why" question is unanswerable. We very rarely know why one person is out and others are still there. The survivors as well as those affected try desperately to find a key or logic to the list, but most often there is none. So if you're in the key performer category, if you're one of those who really made a huge difference at work (saving money, building new systems, bringing in clients, managing complex projects, and so on), you may also have the "why me?" hurdle to get over.

As I talk with my clients about this, I tell them it doesn't make sense, but it happened. It could be part of a game of financial musical chairs because eliminating senior management saves the company more money than divesting itself of lower-level employees. And what I try to get them to think about is the wonderful fact that they are high performers and that they have a track record that is going to help them pitch their abilities to other companies.

Here's what you have to focus on, whether you were with your last company for 25 years or only a few months:

- Your value
- The things you're good at
- Your education
- Your attributes
- Your experience

These are all yours. They don't now and never will belong to a company.

Even if you were a high performer, a favorite, the one who got promoted and was given awards, that doesn't guarantee that you'll be spared when the company cuts back. I understand that this makes it harder because you've identified with the place where you worked, but now is the time to remind yourself that your value hasn't changed. The only thing that's different is your employment status. After all, who has the power to define you: you or your former company?

FIND WAYS TO GAIN PERSPECTIVE

Job loss can be like a huge eraser: It wipes your years of accomplishments off the board and they're gone. Gone forever. But as you define your search goals and construct your resume, you'll be brought face to face with your achievements: the things you did or managed. And if you look over your past performance appraisals (which hopefully accurately reflect your contributions), you'll see that you made a difference. And you'll begin to remember things such as awards, honors, new clients you brought in, classes you designed, and so on.

These are footholds—concrete examples of your value. Read them and reread them. Memorize them. Get yourself to believe that you really did these things, and that in the future, when you get your new job, you'll make similar contributions again.

A client I recently worked with really struggled with this. Her resume was fine, but there was a disconnect: She didn't believe in her own background. When her search went on longer than she had anticipated (at about the three-month mark), she became discouraged and came late to appointments or didn't show up at all. When I asked her what was going on, she laughed—a nervous laugh with no joy in it. I don't know all the details of what turned her around, but after several weeks, she returned to her search with renewed energy and hope. When I asked her about it, she told me that she had quit smoking and had decided to lose weight. She was volunteering once a week at a local soup kitchen. But most importantly, she started every day with gratitude. She sat quietly and thought about what she had rather than what she didn't have. And this helped her get past her panic and move forward.

Quick Do's and Don'ts

Do:

1. Take an inventory of your skills and strengths. Document your assets.

2. Remember what has brought you all this way. Read your past performance appraisals.

3. Realize that work is a contract—not a lifelong commitment. This gives you the freedom to look for new opportunities, leave no-win situations, and manage your own career.

Don't:

1. Expect loyalty from a company. I often try to explain this by looking at the difference between what I call being "smart" loyal and "dumb" loyal (and I know I used to be firmly in the latter category). A person who is "smart" loyal

is dedicated, does his or her job, and makes good decisions about his or her commitments, but understands that it's not the company's business to look after his or her career. A "dumb" loyal worker is wired to be responsible, dedicated, and available no matter what his or her company does or doesn't do. This is often reflexive and unthinking.

2. Feel betrayed. Well, it's okay to feel this in the first few weeks, but then see if you can get beyond it because it will slow you down.

3. Speak poorly about your former company to anyone (except the cat!). This almost always comes back to bite you and can be damaging. That's why your "why I'm no longer with my company" statement must be safe, bland, and neutral. And if you're asked about your former company, say only good things; but of course, stick to the truth. So you could say, "They're going through difficult times, but I had a great opportunity to learn about…." You get the idea.

Resources and Ideas

As you look for ways to reclaim your value and build a strong foundation for your job search campaign, consider a wide variety of resources:

- Join an organization that connects you to people you don't know. The other day, while driving to work, I was listening to NPR and learned about the Chihuahua Club mentioned in Michael Schaffer's book, *One Nation Under Dog*. What caught my ear was how a Chihuahua owner had built a community with other Chihuahua owners by inviting them and their dogs to her place for holiday parties and other events. It might sound silly, but this grew into a strong and effective network.

- Do something you wouldn't ordinarily do. One client threw a huge survivors' party at a local pub when she was downsized. She mostly invited coworkers who had also been let go, but included a few others who were still with the firm. She made it an upbeat and fun event to attend and it immediately strengthened her network. The attendees were grateful for her help and were anxious to help her as well. Her message was loud and clear: "I've lost my job and I'm confident I'll find another one." So she showcased her generosity, creativity, and resilience. Not bad. In addition, she used holiday e-cards to keep her network up to date.

- Start a job seekers' support group if there isn't one in your area. Churches, synagogues, mosques, and community centers will often give you space for free, and the local paper will publish a notice about the meetings. Look for a local outplacement firm (such as the one I work for, Lee Hecht Harrison) and ask whether one of the counselors would come give a talk on resumes, networking, interviewing, or how to get new skills in a difficult job market.

Most of us are happy to volunteer our time. In my experience, the groups that do best have a clear agenda, take advantage of outside resources, don't become complaint groups, and make it easy for members to network with each other.

- Understand that reclaiming your value and networking are intertwined. This isn't a loner's game. Sure, you do many parts of your job search by yourself. But to effectively reclaim your value and move forward, you've got to interact with others. It is through job search conversations that you'll regain confidence and have tangible proof of your value. Others will enrich your search strategies and help you when you get stuck. If nothing else, commit to telling others what you're doing and how it's going.

- And if you're still stuck, at least create a strong presence on LinkedIn, Twitter, Facebook, and other social media. But please make sure you're also getting out of the house. I can guarantee that if you spend the whole day in front of your computer, you will become more frustrated and upset. Take advantage of the wonderful ways we can connect online with others, but don't spend the day alone.

CHAPTER 6

WHEN ONE DOOR CLOSES, ANOTHER MAY HIT YOU IN THE HEAD

Change is tricky. Something new could be happening and you may have a blip of excitement as you hear from a recruiter or get a good networking contact. But then there's the other side. And that could be that you don't want to be in this process and you still resent the fact that you have to look for work. It's like physics, which I really don't understand except for the action-reaction part. So as new things happen, prepare for backlash. Prepare to be tossed back into the early, painful days of job loss.

Some people use a mantra or some kind of personal recognition statement to protect themselves from the emotional backlash. It could be something like *I'm doing a great job on my search and will find work that is satisfying.* I have a friend who told me to repeat this phrase on my way to my first corporate interview: *They'd be lucky to have me.* For others, self protection may come from having something else to focus on, such as volunteering, running, playing tennis, cleaning a closet, or building a new deck. Cooking is good, too. Find the things that work for you and remember that this back-and-forth and up-and-down are just the seesaw effect, and that over time it will even out.

Maybe part of why the job search process is difficult has to do with patience. Patient people and those with long-range vision can see the mess they're in and can also see the way out. As an impatient person, I tend to see the present as lasting forever, but have learned from my clients to trust the process. Trust that one thing leads to another, that one conversation can multiply, and that there are people you don't know today who will be influential in your search.

And another part of this may be the typically American myth that we can pull ourselves up by "our own bootstraps." There's nothing wrong with being fiercely independent; but it's smart to recognize when a little help is a good thing, and that being open to others is not a weakness. It's not something shameful. How you conduct your job search is going to have your fingerprints on it—you need to do it in ways that make sense to you.

But please don't confuse that with doing what comes naturally or feels comfortable. As we all know, we often have to do things outside our comfort zones, and these frequently become the most powerful door openers of all. As you launch your job search, prepare for discomfort and don't let yourself sidestep important progress just because "it feels uncomfortable" or "it isn't natural."

Here's a wonderful phrase that one of my clients liked to use. It captures the essence of this tricky balance between hope and despair, between yes and no. He said, in telling me about an interview that he'd recently had, "I'm cautiously optimistic."

A good thing to aim for is the middle—not wildly up or depressingly down. Each day has a goal and a realistic time period in which to accomplish it. I tell my clients to have a written plan or search map, including titles or job descriptions, location(s), industries, company size, culture, and a list of companies (see appendix C for sample search maps). Along with this you can create a schedule that might include when you'll report to your desk each morning and times for networking calls, research, and answering ads. If it's helpful, include breaks, rewards, lunch with a friend, time to exercise, and so on. You can even use household chores as a balance activity, telling yourself, "I'll answer five ads and then I'll put in a load of laundry" (see appendix A for sample schedules).

SLOW DOWN TO SPEED UP

Let's look at a specific example of a client who got walloped in the head by initial rejection in her search and how she turned herself around. Sarah had a finance and operations background. She was smart and a real go-getter. I suspect that she had learned early on in school how to be successful. But she wasn't one of those people who could skip class and get an A on an exam. She worked. She was methodical. When I met her she had been with a pharmaceutical company for 12 years. She'd been promoted and expected to continue moving up in the company. She had her MBA.

She surprised me by reading every chapter in the manual we give our clients, taking every class, and filling out all the worksheets and exercises. At first I thought this was really wonderful, but then I began to wonder if she was stalling—if all this preparation was a way to avoid jumping in. It wasn't: When she was ready, she began the implementation phase of her search, and again approached this part of the process with energy, intelligence, and dedication.

At about the six-week mark, she got an interview. I helped her prepare for it and asked her to please give me feedback after the interview. She e-mailed me to say that it went well but that she wasn't sure the chemistry was right. When I asked her about this in our next meeting, she couldn't put her finger on it, but felt that the hiring manager wasn't convinced it was the right fit. It was possible that she saw her as overqualified because she had stronger credentials than the job required.

She waited a week and heard nothing. A few days later she sent an e-mail to HR to check where they were in the process. Another week went by and still there was

(continued)

(continued)

no word, so I suggested she e-mail the hiring manager (the person who would be her boss) to see whether she could get an answer. A few days later she received a polite e-mail from the hiring manager stating that she believed my client was over-qualified for the position and that they had selected another candidate.

For the first time in my meetings with her, Sarah was upset and discouraged. She didn't get it. And she was frustrated because she believed in cause and effect: I'll work hard, prepare well, do a good job at the interview, and then be hired. I tried to explain to her that I was confident she did do a good job, but that her efforts didn't guarantee an offer. There are too many variables—too many other factors. And the worst part was, neither she nor I knew what they were. The hiring manager might have decided to hire someone who was referred to the company, or she might have promoted someone from within. Or perhaps the job was put on hold until after a critical meeting. And "overqualified" could be an evasive way of saying "no, thanks," or it could mean that she was too expensive, or that the company was worried that she'd leave after two months. It was hard to say.

What did Sarah do? She took a few days to mope and then made some radical changes. Early in our conversations, I had asked her whether she was open to consulting because she had told me that she was pregnant. She said that she wanted a job like her last one and couldn't see herself as a consultant. However, a consulting firm that she had used in her most recent position kept calling her because they needed her combination of finance and operations expertise as well as her strong pharmaceutical background. So she agreed to interview with them. This led to additional meetings, and before long she had an offer—a really good offer. To top it off, Sarah began to see how exciting this could be and how it would strengthen her network (because she would be calling on many of the major firms in her industry).

She and I went through the offer carefully. She negotiated a few issues and accepted. Before we wrapped up her program, she decided to move and, with her husband, build their dream house. In the course of less than a year, she had changed jobs, changed her role to become a consultant, moved, and had her first child. We've stayed in touch and it's all working. The lesson I learned from her was how valuable that strong foundation was. I'm convinced that her thorough preparation made all that happened afterwards possible and created a buffer to help her through the ups and downs of looking for work. I call this "slow down to speed up."

Quick Do's and Don'ts

Do:

1. Do your best to be cautiously optimistic. To use a cliché, try not to "count your chickens before they're hatched." In other words, if you're called back for a second or third interview with a company, invest some time and effort looking for new leads. Until it's in the bag, you're still in search mode. (Or as one somewhat cynical client put it: "I'll wait to see if my first paycheck bounces before I believe I have a new job.")

2. Try to view change as something that can create new opportunities. This is really difficult if your whole town is in trouble because of a plant closing, but see if you can get training to learn some new skills that could lead to different work. The schools and hospitals should still be open, people still need to get their hair cut and their cars fixed, and you may be able to get funding through unemployment compensation to get the needed skills. (A client I'm working with is an event planner and she's exploring "green events" to be in the forefront of providing environmentally friendly corporate functions.)

3. Ask yourself what you can learn from each experience in your job search. In one interview I had with the second outplacement firm I worked for (having been downsized by the first on my birthday), I assumed that the man interviewing me hated me. His face was like a stone and, no matter how hard I tried, his expression never varied. By the time I got home, I was convinced that the whole thing had been a huge waste of time and effort.

   Two days later, the person in charge of training new hires at the same company called me. He said that the manager who had interviewed me was so impressed that he suggested they hire me without a second interview. To this person's surprise, I burst out laughing, and then quickly had to explain that I was very interested in the offer but hadn't expected it. So what I learned was that I couldn't assume I knew what an interviewer was thinking and that my job was to do my best to listen carefully and answer the questions. I couldn't jump to conclusions about the outcome, especially because some interviewers, like this one, are very difficult to read.

4. Make sure you have a strong foundation for your search because that is one of the best ways to effectively pitch yourself to others and to protect yourself from the inevitable ups and downs of the job search process. Your foundation should include your statements about why you were let go and what you're looking for, a strong resume, accomplishment examples needed for networking and interviews, a spreadsheet of your contacts, a search map that defines your goals, and a daily schedule if that's helpful.

Don't:

1. Assume you're not making progress when the phone doesn't ring. However, make sure you're running a smart search—one that is balanced and uses referrals or connections to get to the person or people who can hire you.

2. Take abuse. Through my clients as well as my own experience, I've encountered rude people who lash out or treat you unprofessionally. If possible, salvage what you can. Maybe this person is someone you know you could never work for, but see if they have industry knowledge or referrals to recruiters that could be helpful. But walk away from or avoid situations that bring you down.

3. Assume that when you go on an interview the people seeing you have read your resume or even have a clear sense of the job description. Many people aren't very good at conducting interviews and sometimes a person is thrown in at the last moment to talk with you, so be prepared to explain your background thoroughly.

Resources and Ideas

A search schedule provides the framework for what you do and when you do it and helps protect you from the ups and downs of the search process. You're not looking for work when you feel like it or only when things are going well. This is a daily commitment. Except for short breaks and rewards, you're not stopping until you have an offer.

- Your networking activities help you maintain balance and momentum as well. You're a one-person public relations machine and keep your contacts up to date. And periodically—it could be each day or once a week—you'll look at your written plan or map as well as your schedule, see the progress you've made, and figure out where you need to focus next.

- Ask yourself, "What's the one thing I can do today that will move my search forward?" This is helpful because it forces you to be intentional and not simply busy. This is a hard process, and it's critical to be smart and continually figure out what will work best.

- Many of my clients look at me strangely when I suggest a search plan and daily schedule. So I ask them, "Would you plan a wedding without a budget, timeline, and to-do list? Did you manage complex projects at work by the seat of your pants?" And then they smile at me, as if I'm a very challenged person intellectually to even suggest such silliness. And while they're smirking, I make the connection to what they need to do now to manage their job search campaigns.

  Why is there this disconnect? Why should it be a surprise that this is a complex task? I think the answer has to do with the fact that many of us haven't had to do this before, so we're coming from ignorance. And as you'll learn in part 2, there's a lot of misinformation about looking for work.

- Watch your expectations because you might expect this search to be just like your last one. It used to be that you could throw together a decent resume, post it on a few sites, get called in for an interview, and within a week or two have a nice offer. And while this still could happen, it's not most people's experience in our current economy.

CHAPTER 7

BEWARE THE INFORMATION AGE

When I started working as a career counselor in 1994, outplacement firms didn't have Internet access. We heard about it, people had personal computers for word processing, but the full force of the "Information Superhighway" hadn't hit yet. As we all know, that soon changed radically and job hunting online became the thing to do. I would never go back to those pre-Internet days because of all the valuable information that is now at our fingertips, but the sheer amount of information also creates a challenge.

As you'll see in the sidebar, posting your resume on Internet job sites (such as Monster, Yahoo! HotJobs, CareerBuilder, Indeed, Dice, and so on) and answering Internet ads isn't a bad thing to do as long as it's balanced with other activities. When it becomes the only way you're searching, when you're spending all day going from one site to another, checking your e-mail, and filling out applications, it's usually painfully slow.

What I've come to realize, in working with hundreds of people of all levels and functions in the job search process, is that the Internet is seductive. Because we can find anything from the best price on a new mattress to a winning recipe for butternut squash soup, we expect instantaneous results. But when it comes to job search, that doesn't usually happen.

Let's say you find an ad, it's perfect for you, it's as if the person who wrote it knew exactly what you're particularly good at and put it in writing. With a blip of excitement you read and reread the ad, craft your cover e-mail, look admiringly at your resume that proves you're the one for this job, and with a smile, you hit the Send button. You put this entry on your spreadsheet or whatever way you keep track of your submissions, and because it's the perfect job—no, because it's *your* job—you highlight it in hot pink, get up from your desk, and wait for the phone to ring.

After a few trips to check what's in the refrigerator, you look at your phone. It must be broken, or maybe a tree fell on the wires, because it's not ringing. So you pick it up, hear the reassuring dial tone, and put it back down. You hum a song, straighten your desk, and decide it's time to take the dog out for a walk. You grab the leash, but then realize if you're outside with traffic sounds or your dog barking, it could be difficult to talk, so you figure you had better stay in. The dog lies down by the door, disappointed in you. You sit back down at your desk and try to get interested in something else, but your mind is like metal filings clinging to a magnet; it just wants this one thing.

The day is endless, the week an eternity, and still the phone doesn't ring. No, it rings but it's the police benevolent society asking for money. And although you appreciate the sacrifice that the police force makes every day for your safety, you're abrupt on the phone and tell the stunned officer that you're out of work and can't possibly contribute the $20 you gave last year.

What should you do? Take advantage of the Internet, answer ads, post your resume on job boards, and gather information on companies you're exploring, but protect yourself in two critical ways: Don't expect instantaneous results, and balance your search so that you're also networking, targeting companies directly, and getting out of the house.

THE INTERNET: FAST AND SLOW

In my first meeting with Pat, I asked her about her goals and what had happened at her previous company. We also discussed her financial timeframe and which classes and other resources would be most useful to her. Then we started working on her resume. Within a week or two, we had her resume completed and I sensed that she was thinking, "Okay, Jean was a big help, but now I don't need her anymore." In my mind we've just started the process, but in hers we're done.

I gave Pat a list of classes to take and asked her to get her references in order, post her resume on a number of sites, respond to ads, and draft her search map. I also mentioned that she needed to create a networking spreadsheet and make sure, in her conversations with others, that she was asking for general information (Web sites, recruiters, professional associations, and so on) and asking her network whether they'd look at her list of companies.

I checked in on Pat a week later and she told me that she was fine and was getting things done. When we hit about the one-month mark in her search, I sensed that something was wrong. So I asked her if she was struggling.

"Well," she said, "I've answered a ton of ads—all a fairly good fit—and I've used the resume that we worked on and a strong e-mail cover letter, and I haven't had one response."

First we discussed whether she thought anything was missing from her resume, but we both came to the conclusion that it was fine. Then we talked about the time warp and realistic expectations for online submissions. In explaining the time warp I told her that when she was working, a day or a week or even two weeks didn't seem like a long time because she was busy and wasn't involved in a highly unpredictable process like job search. And as we talked about realistic expectations, we spoke about the volume of responses that most online ads generate and how difficult it is to be noticed or pulled out of the pile. "In many ways," I told her, "by the time you see a posting, it's too late."

"How can that be?" asked Pat. "Why would companies do that if they're not really looking for strong candidates?"

"What I mean is when you see a posting, so do hundreds if not thousands of other people. If you can network into a company and connect with the hiring manager before he or she gets to the posting stage, you'll have much less competition and be way ahead of the game."

"Jean, I get that, but this job is me. It's written for me. I match everything they want."

"That's good," I told her, "but another challenge is that in many companies HR is sifting through the mountains of resumes that get e-mailed everyday and they might not see that you're a match or recognize your potential. In fact, because of the volume, they may never even see your resume at all."

We concluded our meeting by talking about how she could use the Internet without getting trapped by it. To help her with this, I told her my librarian story. I shared with Pat that at the three outplacement firms I've worked for, we have always had at least one librarian to help clients research the companies they're exploring, and to help them find other useful information. As the Internet became the tool of choice, one of the librarians taught me her "10-minute rule." She had a kitchen timer on her desk, and as she started a search, she set the timer to 10 minutes. Then she clicked from one site to another to find what she was looking for. When the timer went off, she had to stop and consider what she had so far: Was it useful, was it worth continuing, how would this help the client? Depending on the answers, she either stopped and sent what she had found to the client or set the timer for another 10 minutes and continued the search. What this did was prevent mind-numbing information overload and kept the Internet search clearly connected to goals.

Although Pat was still going to use the Internet as a vital part of her search, I hoped that she would learn how to change her expectations so that it didn't trap her. And if she borrowed the librarian's time-management system, she could control how much of her search was spent online and ensure that she had time and energy for other methods of job searching.

Quick Do's and Don'ts

Do:

1. Become familiar with the best Internet job sites. Ask people in your field which ones they've found particularly helpful. Dice, for example, is very strong for IT, while Medzilla is good for the pharmaceutical and biotech industries. And Monster is good for overall exposure, whereas many like Indeed because it gathers information from diverse resources.

2. Post your resume on several sites to give yourself wide visibility. If you need to keep your search confidential, take your name off your resume and create a new e-mail address (that doesn't use your name) just for your search.

3. Use the power of the Internet to do in-depth research on the companies you're interested in. Go beyond their Web sites because if there's negative or controversial information about a company, it sure won't be on the company Web site. Many find the Hoovers (www.hoovers.com) or Dun & Bradstreet (www.dnb.com/us/index.asp) databases helpful.

4. As you create your daily schedule (see appendix A), set aside specific times when you surf the Internet so that online searching doesn't eclipse other efforts. You're an information-gathering machine; but remember, the machine isn't running you. Use the powerful resources of the Internet wisely and you'll be way ahead of most job seekers.

5. Use the services of the reference librarian at your local public library if you get stuck. As far as I'm concerned, these people walk on water and can find anything. (Besides, their help is free.)

Don't:

1. Spend all your time going from one job site to another. Not only is it not productive, but also I guarantee it will make you feel worse than you do already.

2. Confuse the ease of finding information with what works. If you're going to have a new roof put on your house, you can look in the Yellow Pages and surf the Internet to find local roofers, but most people will ask a neighbor so that they're getting indispensable, firsthand information about the roofer. Why pay all that money for someone who did sloppy work or took weeks to complete the job?

3. Let the seduction of the Internet—all those job postings—lull you into believing that this is how you get your finger on the pulse of the job market. It's one source (and a good one to have as part of the mix), but people in your industry, as well as people who know people in your industry, can be equally helpful.

Resources and Ideas

Let's assume that you are like many of my clients and you're still unconvinced. You believe that the Internet is the only way to go. It's how you found your last job—and maybe the one before that. What can you do to find out whether you should be following some of my suggestions?

- Ask people you know how they found their jobs.
- Read a few books on the job search process and get a sense of what experts say. (Several excellent books I've read recently are *Highly Effective Networking: Meet the Right People and Get a Great Job* by my colleague Orville Pierson; *How to Land Your Dream Job: No Resume! And Other Secrets to Get You in the Door* by Jeffrey J. Fox; *Job Search Magic* by Susan Britton Whitcomb; and

60 Seconds and You're Hired! by Robin Ryan. Take a look at appendix H, "Suggested Reading," if you want more ideas.)

- Attend professional association meetings and local job support group meetings and learn from others who are also looking for work. Make sure to ask them how they're generating activity—what's getting them in the door.

- Combine search methods. So if you see an ad that seems perfect, answer it and then look for a contact at that company so that your name gets pulled out of the hundreds of applicants. Search smart and your phone will ring.

CHAPTER 8

NEW IS NOT ALWAYS
WORSE, JUST DIFFERENT

Let's look at something I touched on earlier: the example of a person who has lost a job that he or she hated—as my clients like to put it, "the job from hell." This could be a situation where your boss is demanding, erratic, and otherwise nuts; or it could be that the company culture and expectations are that they own you. It's 7 p.m. on a Friday and you're still at your desk. Or it's Sunday and you're called into the office. You get the picture.

You're stressed, irritable, exhausted, and unhappy, but you have a job. Then you're called into your boss's office and told that you're no longer needed. So now, from my perspective, you have two challenges: finding a new job and recovering from your past one. And you may have to get through the second process before you can run an effective search.

I explain this as detoxifying. You have poison in your system, you're used to poison, poison feels almost natural, and now you have nothing. So although it's a job you hated, you resent the fact that it's been taken away from you. And in some cases you may even believe that the company owes it to you to keep you employed as compensation for your pain and suffering. Anger, the desire for revenge, disbelief, shock, hurt, and who knows what else compete for your attention. You're a mess and you're afraid you'll never have another job. You think there is only this one company, your previous one where you were totally unhappy, that will hire you. No one else will and you can come up with a convincing list of reasons why that's true.

From the outside, or from my perspective as a career counselor, it can seem like a good thing that you're no longer stuck in a job that you hate. But to many of the people I've worked with who have experienced this, it's a double whammy.

Recently I was counseling a client who had felt abused by his most recent job and was struggling to move on. To complicate things, after he was in search mode for about two months, the company offered to rehire him. As we discussed whether he should accept this offer, I made him promise to do some things for himself so that he could manage his career better and not get stuck. I reminded him to try to view work as a contract that can end at any time. He would of course work hard, but had learned that he also needed to balance work with other activities. He promised to join a gym and go at least twice a week. He agreed to keep his resume active on some job boards and to use LinkedIn to keep his network up to date.

He had choices, and by not getting into the "there is only this one company" thinking that had hurt him in the past, he knew he could do a better job of setting reasonable expectations at work. As we ended our time together, I shook his hand and said, "You're the boss. It's up to you to decide where you'll work and what you'll do." He agreed and I was confident that he could return to his former company and make it work.

WHEN THE JOB YOU'VE LOST HAS DAMAGED YOU

Ingrid came to this country as a teenager from Eastern Europe. Her family was hardworking. She helped in her father's store as a child and got her first job at age 16. She always worked and always did whatever her bosses requested of her. Like her parents, she was convinced that this was the way you succeeded. She got a college degree (through scholarships, student loans, and of course working throughout her education) and was hired by a law firm in midtown Manhattan. She was promoted and was known in the company as someone who was entirely reliable.

The work was intense and she did it without complaining. On one project, the deadlines were so challenging that instead of staying late and then commuting back to New Jersey, she brought an air mattress and a blanket to work, slept in her office, and changed her clothes in the ladies' room the next morning. Some days she never left the building.

Despite this selfless work ethic, she lost her job but couldn't understand why. After all she had done, how could they have let her go? And yes, she knew that her company didn't get a key account, but she still saw herself as an essential part of the team that would turn things around. In her mind, the company couldn't function without her. In other words, she believed that she was indispensable.

In our first few meetings I could see that she didn't trust me and that she thought it was highly questionable to even try to create a space between herself and her previous employer. She was them. They had given her an identity. And by listening carefully to the language she used, I could hear that when she said, "I was with XYZ company," what she was really saying was "I am XYZ company."

Most of us would agree that change is difficult but can lead to good things. It can break us out of old patterns and allow us to chart a better course for ourselves. This is the pain and gain syndrome. But from my experience of working with clients like Ingrid, I have found that this isn't always the case.

Ingrid couldn't let go—she couldn't see herself anywhere except working for her former company. She went through the motions of running a job search, but her heart wasn't in it. By the time her program was over, she had put some of her energy into volunteering at her daughter's school, but other than that, she had given up on working again. I am not a psychologist, and I do my best to be

(continued)

(continued)

careful not to give advice outside of my expertise, so I can't explain all the reasons why she was unable to move on. What I can say with certainty is that here was a person with great talent and a wonderful work ethic who hadn't learned how to protect herself or to see that she and the company she worked for were separate.

Quick Do's and Don'ts

Do:

1. Make a careful inventory of the resources available to you that will support your search. If you're not sure where to begin and you don't have an outplacement program, call HR at your former company to ask for suggestions, register with the unemployment office and ask about classes, check your local paper for job search support groups, use Google to see what's out there, and ask your local reference librarian for help—regarding both groups and other resources.

2. Think of a friend (it could be a former coworker who was also let go) who would make a good search buddy. Ask whether you can team up and call each other once a day to report progress. Maybe you can also decide to meet once a week.

3. Keep a journal if writing helps you think through things. Jot down how you're feeling as well as the things you need to do that day.

4. Educate your family and friends that you have a job: looking for a new job. This will take time, energy, and resources and it's critical that you not be interrupted every 10 minutes because "you're not working."

Don't:

1. Go it alone. Well, if you want to maintain a high level of frustration and drag out your search, then it's a good choice. But most studies show that job seekers who are connected to others land better jobs more quickly.

2. Expect that this is going to be a predictable process. Don't confuse effort with controlling results. You're going to work hard and run a smart search, but that doesn't guarantee that you also know exactly what will happen or when the phone will ring.

3. Let the lack of control bring you down. You can control the actions you're taking and can work on your attitude toward this endeavor. Try to anticipate that there will be difficult times that you will then be creative about getting through.

4. Work nonstop on your job search. Take breaks, get out of the house, check out the free events in your community, and so on. One client got his new job by going bike riding with a friend. The friend introduced him to one of his friends and that led to a job offer.

Resources and Ideas

When I think about change, I often remember the Taco Bell commercial with the slogan, "Change is good." But for many of us, it doesn't feel that way, especially if the change is something as devastating as losing your job. What might help you get through the initial stress and discouragement of this kind of radical change?

- Understand that job loss is part of the culture we live in. It happens frequently to thousands of people. It is not a reflection of your work ethic, your work history, or your personal attributes.

- Use this time when you hopefully have resources to support you (severance, unemployment, and perhaps an outplacement program, classes, or additional training) to do some career planning. As you look at the job market, consider what you enjoy doing and what feels exciting. See if you can focus on those kinds of roles.

- Get to know yourself, whether by reading a book such as *What Color Is Your Parachute?*, which has numerous exercises to help you identify your strengths and interests, or by brainstorming with a friend. Make lists of the things you're good at, your top accomplishments, and what really engages you at work.

- Ask for outside help if you're feeling stuck and can't get past the emotional hurdles of job loss. Figure out whose advice will be most helpful and ask for time to talk.

- Keep in mind that where you are now—if you're struggling and your phone isn't ringing—will change. Nothing helps more than interest from a new company or recruiter, a good interview, or a productive networking conversation. In other words, progress in your search will heal you and help you get past the difficult times.

CHAPTER 9

COURAGE IS KEEPING AT IT

If you ask the average person what courage is, they might say something like "moving ahead despite difficult circumstances." Or as a popular book of the late 1980s put it, *Feel the Fear and Do It Anyway.* And in some cases we have romantic ideas of courage, such as the parent who rushes into a burning building to save their child. Most people don't think of courage when talking about the job search process. Because there are so many misconceptions about what it takes to land a new job, many people think it's an easy endeavor.

Here's what I tell my clients: This is a slippery process where cause and effect may feel as if they've been tossed out the window. Looking for a job can make you feel as if you're looking into a trick mirror that distorts everything. And here's another surprise: The effort it takes to run a good job search is often much more intense than work itself. In other words, you now have a job (looking for work) that is more challenging than the job you just lost. So now you've got an unpredictable process that's exhausting. And while we're at it, let's look at time, which somehow has morphed into an enemy. When you were working, you never had enough time, but now it hangs on you like a heavy burden.

Here's how the day goes: You don't set your alarm. What's the point? You have nowhere to go and can't enjoy the time off because you're afraid to spend any money. Unless you have small children or a demanding dog, you can get up when you feel like it, which is really never. So after tossing around for a while, you stagger out of bed, make breakfast, and think about getting dressed. Everyone in your neighborhood has left for work and it's quiet—really quiet. So then you get the brilliant idea that you should check your e-mail and some of the job boards, answer a few ads, and contact recruiters.

Your e-mail is full of junk, and answering the ads requires effort that you don't feel up to today. You flip from one site to another and look at the clock and see that it's only 10 a.m. The quiet is beginning to get to you and you look out your window with envy at the crew mowing your neighbor's lawn (or if you live in a city, you wish you were anyone walking by on the sidewalk because they clearly have a purpose). Then you think about getting dressed.

You put on an old pair of jeans and a ripped T-shirt and are then embarrassed when UPS comes to your door with a package, because your hair is all matted down and you look like a slob. The package is something you ordered when you were still working, and you decide not to open it because you'll clearly have to return it anyway now that you can't afford anything. You sit back down at the computer with your second cup of coffee, and panic wells up inside you. You are going to die—right now, hands limp on the keyboard, head collapsed on an unwanted copy of your resume.

Here's where courage comes in. You clearly can't stay in this unproductive phase. So first recognize that your world has been turned upside down and you are like a child learning to walk. Accept that you'll be more effective if you get guidance to help you learn new skills. This is where a career counselor and other resources come in. Secondly, realize that you do have an important job and really are CEO, COO, book-keeper, and everything else for your company of one. But, as a teenager might put it, "You have a job but the pay sucks." Pay or no pay, it is a job—and a critical one, at that, because most of us can't afford to give up and not work.

You have to build some structure and predictability into this quirky process to combat these negative feelings. And you need to search smart so that you make progress and can recognize signs of moving ahead.

GET READY TO ACTIVELY FACE DIFFICULT AND UNFAMILIAR FEELINGS

On a gray day in November, I brought a young man in his early thirties into my office for his initial visit. He seemed upbeat and didn't look upset. Oh boy, I said to myself, an easy one. He was in marketing and had relocated to New Jersey after he lost his job on the West Coast. When I asked him why he came to this area, he explained that he and his wife were living with his parents until he found another job. They had one young child. We talked about his goals and past salary. We went over short- and long-term plans. I asked him whether there were any obstacles that I should know about. Nope. Everything was fine.

We completed his resume and worked on networking and interviewing. Before long, he got an interview with a small, local firm. He researched the company, we practiced common interview questions, and he felt confident that he could ace this. I called him the day after the interview to see how it went. "Okay," he said, his voice sounding uncertain.

"Did something go wrong?" I asked.

"No, it's just that they were hard to read. And I was nervous, so I'm not sure I came across as a really good fit."

I couldn't imagine why anyone wouldn't hire this young man—he was bright, good with people, and such a nice person.

"Do you think they thought you might be bored and would leave?"

(continued)

(continued)

"No. I just didn't get a great feeling."

By the time we met the following week there was no news, so we discussed other companies and his overall search strategy. But a week later he got a call telling him that they decided to hire someone else. He was crushed and it occurred to me that he would have to be disappointed because he felt the pressure of providing for his family and didn't want to impose on his parents.

More weeks went by and we had the strategy talk. This means that he had to come up with a list of companies where he'd like to work—not based on openings—and then systematically find contacts inside those companies so that he could work his way to the hiring managers.

The way I put it is this: You're in research mode. You're not asking other people to find you a job, but you are asking whether they know anything about these companies. If they ask you why, your answer is, "These are companies that I believe would be a good fit for my background and skills. What I'm doing is reaching out to people who work for these companies so that I can get a better sense of their needs and industry trends."

At a low point in this process, when he didn't believe that anyone would ever hire him again, he tried to get any kind of job working at the local mall. When that didn't work out, he really panicked. But then he had to commit to the seemingly slow process of networking, which often is much faster than Internet postings or walking into the mall to fill out an application.

And now we're back to courage because this is an example of facing something you hate (being out of work) and making radical changes. You can't do what you feel like doing. You can't turn your brain off. You've got to be smart and strategic in this process.

So what happened to my marketing client? He learned how to network. He reached out to others. He joined a professional association and also took a course to enhance his marketing skills. And through these efforts he found a company that needed someone with his skills, and he's happily working there. Actually, he was hired first on a contract basis for six months. But at about the four-month point they realized how good he was and offered him a permanent position. So now he and his family have their own home again and he's keeping his network active because he understands that his network, not his job, is his safety net and will help him when he's looking for work again.

Quick Do's and Don'ts

Do:

1. Make a list of the resources you'll need to work on to be successful in your job search. These might include learning how to network, organizing your contact list, creating a LinkedIn profile and building your online professional network, finding professional organizations in your field, and so on.

2. Think of a time you got through something really difficult. How did you do it? What helped you?

3. Find people who inspire you—either local people who are doing things you admire or famous people who have overcome adversity. Reading biographies can be one way to go. If you want to learn about a person who overcame terrible hardship, read about Abraham Lincoln.

4. Keep in mind that this is a process made up of a lot of small steps. You don't have to do anything terrifying or huge, but you do need to commit to the small steps that will create interest in your background and get you to your goal.

Don't:

1. Give up before you begin. If you haven't run a really good search and given it time to work, you can't say, "I'll never work again." (This is not to ignore the fact that many communities have been really hard hit. But sometimes you can be part of the solution. In other instances, you may have to look for work in other locations.)

2. Surround yourself with people who bring you down. These are the ones who repeat many times a day: "There are no jobs out there." When I hear this phrase I think, "Here's a person who is isn't willing to try and who doesn't want me to try to find a job because if I do and I succeed, then it would prove he's wrong."

3. Confuse effort with controllable or visible results. The chances are pretty good that you'll find a job, but probably not exactly when or in the way that you want. This is tricky: making a smart effort everyday to get closer to being hired—and simultaneously understanding that there are many factors in this process out of your control. One client told me recently that when she was turned down for a job and called the hiring manager to get feedback, she was told, "We decided to fill that spot from the company we just acquired, rather than the outside." So this still stung, but now she was able to see that there was nothing wrong with what she did. Someone else had an advantage.

Resources and Ideas

So, what can you do today? How can you begin? Make a list of what you think your most critical needs are. This might include

- Getting your resume into shape.
- Registering for unemployment.
- Checking out health benefits through COBRA or other providers.
- Starting a list of contacts.

- E-mailing your references to make sure they're comfortable with serving in this capacity and that they will say good things about you. It's a good idea to also send them your updated resume.
- Not getting trapped by the Internet or your e-mail accounts.
- Putting on your calendar something you can look forward to. This could be lunch with a friend, a movie date, or an hour or two browsing in a bookstore.
- Building momentum. This again is where courage comes in. You may not feel like doing any of the preceding suggestions, but you've got to take action. When you start seeing results, this will become much easier.
- Remembering that courage isn't the absence of fear. It's moving on despite it—or perhaps with it.

CHAPTER 10

MAKING PROGRESS

My mother used to say, when talking about a challenge of any kind, "one step forward and 15 back." That's what I mean about finding your way. Progress is hard to perceive at times. It can feel like you're sinking or going backwards. Your former job (or the one you may still have but are about to lose) pulls on you like gravity—or quicksand. This force makes it difficult to realize that there is anything beyond it. But there is. It may not be visible or immediately knowable, but it's out there waiting for you.

So now, perhaps, the shock of your job loss is lessening a bit. It sure doesn't feel like fun, but hopefully you're adjusting. You're seeing that you can get through this. And although it still stings when you talk to someone from your former company, you realize that there are hours every day during which your focus is elsewhere. This is a great sign and true progress.

Here's an interesting thing—actually this is one of the most common phrases I hear when I tell clients that they're doing a good job: "But I don't have a job yet." If we fast-forward to the time when they're gainfully employed again, and I check to see how this new job is going, many clients say something like, "It's okay. I'm glad for the income and benefits but...." And what they say next tells me that it's not perfect and it doesn't make their other problems go away. In other words, it's only a job. So try to remember not to idealize being employed. It's important, but don't turn it into something it never was or will be.

To judge how you're doing in a complex process by the end result is twisted. It would be like saying, after completing high school, "I obviously didn't learn anything from the past four years because I didn't get the scholarship to Harvard." As I'm working with my clients, I try to wean them from this all-or-nothing thinking and get them to see signs of moving ahead each week. Okay, these can be subtle, but that doesn't mean they're not real. Examples of moving ahead include

- Getting your resume done and getting feedback on it so that you know it does a good job of representing your background

- Organizing your networking list and rereading it frequently because this will help you remember additional contacts
- Joining a professional association or two and attending meetings
- Ordering business cards to make it easy to connect with others (You can get free ones from Vistaprint.com or pick up card stock at an office-supply store and make them yourself—see appendix E for examples.)

These things are real and they're progress. They're not a job offer, but they're steps in the right direction. And that, I believe, is the key to finding your way.

And yes, you'll get lost, too. There will be times when a strong lead peters out; when someone you were convinced would be really helpful won't return your calls; when the interviewers are unprepared and basically waste your time. Understanding how hiring works and then building the skills to effectively pursue your job search is critical. Most career experts agree that hiring happens in three basic ways:

- **The published job market:** This is where a manager at a company has a need (maybe someone got promoted or left) and they post the job on their company Web site or other sites or give the posting to recruiters. Tons of applications get sent in and then someone at the company has to sort through the avalanche. (This is often done by HR.) Eventually they get the list down to a small number. Then they either go through phone screenings to further reduce the list or bring the final candidates in for interviews. Once the top candidate has been selected and his or her references are checked (plus, he or she has passed the drug screening and background checks), the candidate is offered the job.
- **The created job:** In this situation, usually as you're networking and talking with decision makers or hiring managers (in other words, with the person who has the power to hire you), they realize that you have exactly what they need to fix their current problem or challenge. And so, with no competition reducing your odds, a job is created. This obviously happens only when at least three things align: the company's needs, your skills, and their budget.
- **Being known to hiring managers:** This one is a bit like the preceding item, except that a job isn't created for you, but at some point (this could be right away or several months later) one of the hiring managers you've spoken with (hopefully in person) remembers you and realizes that she can save herself a huge headache and a fair bit of money by bringing you in. Ideally you contact these decision makers just before they realize that they need you, but that's hard to determine. The search strategy here is to network to get to hiring managers because conversations with them (these often aren't interviews) are the most productive thing you can do in your search.

We've looked at things you can do to make progress and we've reviewed the ways hiring happens. One last piece of the puzzle is understanding the new work contract and the fact that many of us will not only have different jobs, but will also have several careers in the course of our working lives.

Few people's careers follow a straight line. The exceptions to the rule are the ones who knew when they were 10 years old that they were going to be an accountant or a doctor and their lives from then on moved methodically in that direction. The rest of us are interested in things, go to college (or not), and through a series of coincidences or quirky luck end up in a job that then leads to other jobs—sometimes in the same field and sometimes not.

Gone are the days of long-term employment—of the big companies that loved hiring people right out of school and training, retaining, and promoting them. The second time I was downsized, my boss (as part of his goodbye speech) told me that employment is a contract. It's not forever. (I was so upset that all I could do was wonder why he dyed his hair jet-black and why he didn't realize that it made him look older.) But later, when I had settled down and was actively interviewing with that company's competitors, I realized he was right. It is a contract. And it's my job to take care of my career. It's my responsibility to make sure my skills and resume are up to date, that my network keeps me visible in my field, and that I'm ready, at a moment's notice, to jump back into the search process.

When I share this story with my clients, they often look sad and say that they think this is a terrible way to live. They want the gold watch that their mother or father received after 35 years with one company. I try to explain to them that the work contract has shifted and, like it or not, we've got to deal with it. But there's also a freedom in this new way of working, which is that we can leave a job if it's not right. We're our own advocates. We're making decisions that will be best for us. I can't tell you how liberating it is to many clients who have worked for one company to realize that, as they put it, "there's life outside my previous company." Choices are a good thing.

YOU'VE GOT CHOICES

Here's an example of a client who managed to see his job search as an adventure. We'll call him Ravi. He was from India but he'd been in this country a long time and had a wonderful job with a major manufacturing company. He was up to date in his field, which was Quality Assurance. Then he lost his job. After a quick adjustment to being out of work, Ravi told me that his game plan was to go after everything.

"Everything?" I asked.

"Well, what I mean is any good job anywhere."

"So you'd move to Texas if you got an offer?" (He lived in New Jersey.)

"I'm not sure. But I figure it doesn't hurt to go through the interview process to see what happens."

So we agreed that this was fine and he proceeded to answer ads, network, attend his professional association meetings, expand his LinkedIn connections, contact

(continued)

(continued)

recruiters, and use his list of possible employers (the most important part of your search map) to get connected to hiring managers. Not long after that, Ravi told me that he had an interview in Connecticut. We both knew that it was too far for a daily commute, but he decided not to worry about it. A few weeks later, he found out that he wasn't selected.

Next he flew out to California to interview with a biotech firm. He told me that his wife thought it was a bit far as he wouldn't even be able to come home most weekends. But he again decided just to do it. Before he heard back from them, he finally had a local interview. When we debriefed from it, he told me that the company was too small and not very well run, but that if they made him an offer, he'd accept it and keep looking.

This was huge—it was amazing—because he was with his former company for 25 years. He had radically changed his way of thinking about work and was making the search process creative and open. I'm sure that the people interviewing him sensed this, too. He was not desperate, not depressed, and certainly not afraid. He had a "here I am; take it or leave it" attitude. I told him I wished I could bottle this and share it with others. He accepted the local job and had realistic expectations about it and didn't need to make it more than it was. I was confident that with this attitude he would be fine and that if the new job didn't work out, he would know how to find another one. Ravi had learned the freedom of choices and understood work as a contract.

Quick Do's and Don'ts

Do:

1. Think about what you want for your career. If you're young and have lots of options in front of you, you might want to invest time in working through some career planning. Reading *What Color Is Your Parachute?* and working with your school's career development office are great resources for helping you with this. (And keep in mind that you don't have to be a current student. Most alumni can also use these resources.)

2. If you're under financial pressure and you need a job quickly, figure out your easiest path. Most career counselors will tell you that going after the same function in the same industry is usually the quickest route to a new opportunity. This changes, however, if either your industry or function has been wiped out. So someone in Michigan who has worked in car manufacturing could have a tough time because their industry is in trouble, as could a Wall Street trader, whose function has been virtually eliminated.

3. Get help in sorting through your options and plan. Sharing, brainstorming, and getting outside advice almost always help you clarify your ideas and are good ways to avoid dead ends. As an example, I had a client who wanted to be a teacher, but my sense of her was that she was a quiet person who might be

exhausted by being in front of a boisterous group of kids all day. I suggested she shadow a teacher (a friend who taught elementary education) for a few days so that before she made a huge investment, she'd at least have a sense of what it's like to teach in a school. This small effort saved her years of going down the wrong path; she decided that was not what she was best suited for.

Don't:

1. Jump into a complex process without planning. Panic is not your friend. Having a strong foundation and the materials you need to support your search will make you more successful.

2. Tell people that you'll "take anything." This is a depressing message. One of the great ironies of job searching is that people don't want to help people who sound desperate.

3. Get ahead of yourself. This is a one-moment, one-effort-at-a-time endeavor. Things can change quickly. Where you are today in terms of the responses you're receiving can shift in an instant. Look at your plan or search map, work it, keep to your search schedule, reward yourself, and you'll get there.

Resources and Ideas

What else will help you make progress? How do you know how you're doing?

• Look at your implementation timeline (appendix G), which gives you a snapshot of your critical deadlines. If you know, for example, that you need to be bringing in income within the next few months, you might be ready to consider your plan B (appendix D) so that you're already working on other ways to earn money.

• Ask your search buddy, or someone whose opinion you think will be helpful, to review your search with you. What's most important here is to analyze what has been working and what may not be getting you results, and then adjust your strategy so that you're doing more of the things that are effective. Let's say you're spending half your time on the Internet answering online ads but haven't had a single response. You could decide to cut that time in half and instead reach out to recruiters, sign up with some contract firms or employment agencies, and set a quota for yourself each day so that you talk with at least five people.

• Remember, as you evaluate your search, that it's really important to focus on the things that make you feel better. The catch here is that they might be the things you're avoiding. At the top of this list is networking—almost every client I've partnered with is amazed to discover that these conversations lift their spirits and remind them of their strengths and abilities. So make the calls, invite people to join you for coffee, and attend meetings. You'll not only be getting others' help in this critical endeavor, but you'll also feel better.

- Choices and progress are related. You can't afford to get stuck, day in and day out, doing the same things if you're not reaching your goals. Ask yourself, "What else can I do? Who do I know who seems to be getting better results in their search?" And then see if they'll share their strategy with you.

CHAPTER 11

HAVE INSURANCE FOR A TRICKY PROCESS

The best insurance you can "buy" for the challenging task in front of you—looking for a new job—is to run a smart search. This doesn't mean that your search will necessarily be quick and easy, but it does mean that you'll get there. And along with a smart search, it's a good idea to build a safety net that can help you if things get rough or if your search goes on longer than anticipated.

When I was making a huge transition in my own career from nonprofit work to a corporate job, I got stuck. The vast majority of companies that fit my criteria (they were in New York City where I was living at the time, they were in training, and they offered courses in communications—particularly writing—where I had some credibility and experience) weren't hiring. They were too small. They were one- or two-person firms and probably didn't have enough work for themselves, let alone another person.

At last I found a major firm but now had new obstacles: I didn't know anyone there, and my network—two people in particular—gave me specific reasons why I wouldn't want to work for this company. One said that I'd have to be an account executive and sell programs, not just deliver them; and the other had all kinds of stories about how awful the company was. So I filed them away and kept getting nowhere. As the Christmas season hit, I realized that I had to do something because I was beginning to question myself—wondering whether there was something wrong with me, or if, in some crazy way, I really didn't want to work. So I came up with a plan B: a retail job in a flower shop. I had worked in one as a teenager and my knowledge of flowers wasn't bad.

I walked up Broadway and went into several shops asking to speak to the manager. I didn't tell them how many years it had been since I'd worked in this industry, but simply offered to help them out during a busy season. I got hired. The salary was awful, the work hard, and my lunch break unpaid. It didn't matter—I had a job. I took thorns off roses, carted huge pots of poinsettias around, answered questions from shoppers, wrapped bouquets, swept the floor, and basically did the work that no one else wanted to do. I had a paycheck, I had purpose, I had something tangible to do every day, and I even got a 30 percent discount at the shop, which I used for my holiday shopping.

At the same time, I realized I had to get a better job. I needed to use my college education and needed to do something more challenging that also paid better. So, one morning, before going to work, I decided to call the large firm that my two friends had told me to avoid. A few weeks earlier I had found the name of the hiring manager (through a professional association I had joined) and I had sent him my resume. Nothing happened. With my resume in front of me and pen in hand, I dialed his number. He answered his phone and I told him that I was following up on the resume I had sent him and that I was very interested in training opportunities at his firm.

There was a long pause and then he said, "Can you come in now?"

"Sure," I answered. "Is it okay if I'm there in an hour?"

He said it was fine, told me which floor to come to, and hung up.

Now I was in full panic mode. I called the flower shop and told them I'd be late. I ran down the hall to my neighbor's to see if I could borrow a suit; but she had already gone to work, so I went through my closet and found the most corporate dress I could find. I fixed my hair, did my makeup, and ran out of the building. I hailed a cab and in about 20 minutes I was at the office.

Heart pounding, I went up to the 45th floor and told the receptionist who I was and who was expecting me. She took my coat and offered me coffee, and I waited. As I was sitting there, I looked around and noticed that the office was bright, nicely decorated, and lively. People were talking in the halls. I thought it would be really fun to work here. Finally, the receptionist took me to the manager's office. We shook hands and he closed the door.

Two things saved me: One of my credentials was that I had taught a remedial course in expository writing at NYU—where he went to college. The other was that I'm a good listener. This interview is what I later called my "un-huh" interview because I nodded, made little affirmative noises, and barely got a word in. I don't know what he saw in me, but perhaps it was that I was eager to join this company and could learn quickly. At the end of the interview he asked if I'd like a tour of the office and I knew that was a good sign. By the time I was back on the street, I was grinning. I wouldn't know for another two weeks (the day after New Year's Day) that I had the job, but I knew I had done alright. I knew I had a chance. And it was so exciting. I dashed home, changed into my jeans, and buzzed around the flower shop like a madwoman.

This may not be true, but in my mind being willing to take the flower shop job opened the way to the corporate one—not in a literal way, but more in proving to myself that I wanted to work, could work, and would find a job. So in addition to income, a plan B can help because it reconnects you to work and allows you to take a break from full-time job searching. It may also help by connecting you to new skills and people.

Your safety net is a smart search and some fallback plans. And it's also including others in the process so that you're not alone and can benefit from other points of view. That's what will help you keep from getting stuck.

SEARCH SMART

Joe was a senior finance professional. He had lost his job two years ago, found a new one, and believed that he'd never have to go through this process again. But one day, as I came into the office, there he was. He rolled his eyes at me and said, "Here I am again."

I wanted to say, "Oh, no!" but didn't want him to feel unwelcome. So I simply asked, "What happened?"

He told me about the job and how much he had enjoyed it. But the company was acquired by another company, and we all know the rest of that story. Joe knew what to do—he was an excellent job seeker. And of course, he had been through this process recently. We did a little work on his resume. He put together his game plan, but he had a hard time coming up with a list of companies to target.

When we talked about this he said, "I just want a job." I figured we'd see how this strategy would go and refine it if necessary.

A few months went by and he was still upbeat, although I sensed that some of this was a show put on for my benefit. When I asked if he was discouraged, he said, "No," and clearly didn't want to talk about it.

Before long he got interviews at two companies. In the first one, he was a bit rusty and didn't feel that he sold himself effectively. But by the second, he was more confident. Both companies politely turned him down. Now he was in full panic mode. Severance had run out, unemployment didn't cover his expenses, and he told me he'd take "anything." He cancelled his meeting with me but sent me an e-mail telling me that he was exploring working as a financial advisor.

This was a huge departure. It was basically a sales position in which he would be calling on people to try to get them to use the company's services for financial planning. The problem was that he had no sales background or training. There was a promise of money (although it was 100 percent commission based), and my question was whether this was something he could succeed in. Would what the company told him he could earn and what he would really earn even be close?

Despite talking to another client who had also been approached by the same financial planning organization, Joe decided that this was his only option. He had given up on finding a senior finance position, and chose a plan B that was highly speculative. I don't know if this has worked out for him, but I was worried that he would end up in a worse financial situation. What might have helped? What could you do if you're in a similar place?

First of all, I think it's important to have a plan B ready well before you need it. Desperation doesn't lead to good decisions. So as you start your job search, come up with a secondary plan for earning money that's a bit easier to achieve than your

(continued)

(continued)

plan A. One of my clients years ago became a limousine driver as his plan B. What was very cool about this was that he got to drive top executives to the airport, and of course he chatted with them. In the front passenger seat he just happened to have a stack of his resumes handy, so as they offered to help him, he could give them one. Another client delivered newspapers. Because it was the holiday season, he made several thousand dollars from tips.

Secondly, looking back on Joe's story, the outcome might have been quite different if he had been willing to create a list of companies to pursue early in his search. By sharing this list with others, he could have gained inside contacts, which even if they don't lead to an interview or offer, almost always provide industry information and additional leads. From my perspective, Joe was avoiding the most productive activity in the search process: what most people call networking.

Quick Do's and Don'ts

Do:

1. Create a plan B. Know how you can bring in some income if your search takes a while. See what others have found helpful, talk with a counselor at unemployment, and think back to work you've done before so that you have several ideas to pursue.

2. Monitor the way you're looking for a job. Make sure you're not addicted to one method. If you're having trouble networking, for example, ask someone to help you. When you search "smart," you're much more likely to get good results.

3. Review what you've accomplished each week and make a list of your top priorities for the next week. This will help you make sure you do what's most critical, not what's easiest.

4. Know how you'll get around obstacles that are common for this tricky process. The things that have challenged some of the clients I've worked with include never having looked for work before, intolerance of the search process, an unwillingness to learn about it, depression, blind dedication to a former company, huge generalizations such as "big pharma is a mess," lack of a support system, poor time-management skills, and a mistrust of those trying to help them.

Don't:

1. Wait until your back is to the wall to figure out some alternative ways to bring in income.

2. Assume you know what is going to work in your job search. Even those of us who see thousands of searches a year are continually surprised.

3. Let discouragement stop you for long. Setbacks are real and difficult to get through, but you can't let them stop you.

4. Ignore your search map and schedule. In these documents you've defined your search—including the critical list of companies—and you've created a schedule that you need to follow. Your commitment is that you must do the things each week that you've set out to do.

Resources and Ideas

This might be a good time to review the resources and ideas lists in the previous chapters and see what you've had a chance to try and what you may still want to consider. However long you've been in the search process, can you point to specific ways in which you've made progress? Are you moving from shock, denial, anger, and disbelief into some steps that move you forward?

- If you're keeping a journal, go back to your first entries and notice how you've changed. If you're working with a career counselor or search buddy, ask them what they notice about you that's different.

- What can you measure—what facts can provide a foothold to help you see your own progress? On the teams that we run at Lee Hecht Harrison, we measure the time each job seeker spends on their search each week, the number of e-mails they send, and who they've talked with—on the phone or in person. The bull's-eye of this last category is conversations with hiring managers because they are the ones who have the power to make hiring decisions.

- Read a book or listen to a podcast that enhances your search skills. Visit your local library or bookstore or take a look at the "Suggested Reading" list in appendix H.

- Ask someone you admire whether they've ever been through this process and how they got their next job. Make sure to ask them about the techniques that they found effective and whether they had a plan B or have any other ideas that made their search easier to sustain.

- Most importantly, don't give up before you begin. The economy we're currently in is challenging, but hiring is happening. I see it every day, as do my colleagues. You need only one job. As I like to tell my clients, "At least you don't have the president's job—trying to turn around the whole economy. All you need is to find one job where your skills and abilities match what the company needs." And for some this may involve retraining and a radically new career direction, while others will find a job quite similar to their last one.

- Remember, you have to go through this process only once. When I tell my clients this, I see disbelief in their faces and then I explain: You will go through this only once unprepared. Only this time are you having to build new muscles and learn new skills. Once you have them, they're yours. You'll keep them with you and they'll serve you if and when you're thrown into this process again. But only once will it feel like being flattened by a speeding truck. Only once will you not know what to do. Only once will you be scared and lost. So if this feels difficult, tell yourself you have to do it only once. And with the knowledge and skills you gain, you can help others as well as yourself, and subsequent searches will be easier. This is particularly true for those who keep their network active.

IN HER OWN WORDS: LIKE A DIVORCE

I was the typical "dedicated employee." I followed in my father's footsteps into a large pharmaceutical company and had celebrated when I was recognized for my accomplishments. Dad retired after 40 years with the company, and I figured I would do the same. I had already finished 24 ½ years there, and I didn't see any major obstacles to staying for another 10 or 15.

I had been out of the office for several weeks because of the holidays and my mom's death. I returned to the office on a Monday and stayed late to catch up on the e-mails that had invaded my inbox. I finally left around 7 p.m. and drove home. I had heard through the grapevine that the next day would be started with a round of layoffs, but other than the "normal" dread that sort of news generated, I wasn't overly concerned. My project was high on the strategic initiatives list.

The next morning, at about 8:30 a.m., my phone rang. It was for a meeting in a conference room in another part of the building. My heart sank, for that could mean only one thing. Strategic project or not, I wasn't going to see my 25th service anniversary with the company. I slowly walked down to the room where my boss's boss and an HR representative waited.

That was a little over five years ago, and I can still remember a number of details of that day. I know what shirt I was wearing. I know that I apologized when I broke down a bit and explained, "My mom just died last week, and my emotions are a bit raw." I know that my name was misspelled on my severance folder and remember them carefully explaining that I wasn't a victim of age discrimination. I remember being ushered to the next room, where a representative of an outplacement service waited to introduce his firm and their services. I remember nothing of that conversation.

I walked back to my desk, where facilities had thoughtfully delivered boxes for me to pack my personal belongings. A close friend was there waiting for me, and she helped me sort through papers and stuff. Charlotte found a cart and we loaded my car. Somewhere along there, I called my husband. I found my boss and discovered that he, too, was packing his office, as was a third member of my team. We exchanged personal e-mail addresses, and I made my way to the cafeteria for a "last lunch." I was numb. I can remember that Charlotte and I sat in one of the booths, and I watched a squirrel run up one of the trees outside, but I have no idea what time I left the building.

After lunch, I undocked my laptop and walked into the office of my boss's boss. I handed him the laptop and my employee badge. Again I apologized about my display of emotions (sniffles and a few tears), and he said nothing. Absolutely nothing. I walked out, thanked Char, and drove home.

John was there when I opened the door, and he enveloped me in a giant bear hug. "I told Lenny that I'd be out the remainder of this week, if you want me to." At that point, I didn't know what I wanted. We decided to go for a ride, and ultimately ended up in south Jersey at a favorite sushi place. After dinner, we stopped by my sister's house (in the same town) to fill her in. I had left a message for her somewhere along the line saying simply, "I was laid off. Don't call; I don't want to try to explain."

The next morning, the alarm rang at the "usual" time. I don't remember if John stayed home with me that day, or if I sent him to work. I do know I sent him to work by Thursday. I wanted to wallow at home on my own. By Thursday, I started to draft a resume based on what I had remembered from my original 1981 job hunt. I sat down at my computer and posted that resume to Monster.com. In addition, I started reading job descriptions. After a morning or two of that, I couldn't keep straight which ones I wanted to apply to, so I started writing down where I had applied. I started to pay attention to the keywords in the descriptions. I talked to my lawyer and signed my severance package. I cried. I felt lost and hollow.

I filed still more applications. No calls. I started to feel as though I had no value. Who would want me, anyway? I didn't have the latest and greatest certifications, I wasn't technical anymore—why would they want me? More applications went out; no responses came back in. I was spending more and more time in front of the computer. I didn't feel as though I could go anywhere or do anything because I might miss that "perfect" posting.

Somewhere during the last week of January, after I had been home about two-and-a-half weeks, I answered the phone to hear the voice of my assigned "outplacement counselor." I don't remember the specifics of that call, but I did sense calmness in Jean's voice, and something said that I could trust her for guidance. I decided that I would give this a try. We set an appointment for a week or so out.

More applications, and more nothingness, filled that week. With self-esteem about as low as it can get, I changed out of my jeans and flannel shirt and drove over to Jean's office. After the initial paperwork, I was met by a dynamo who ushered me back to her office. I tried to assess what I was up against, as she briskly introduced me to the program. Classes. A new resume. Regular team meetings. Available cube space. Phones. Faxes. Resources. My head was spinning.

I left that afternoon with a book under my arm detailing the steps to finding a new job, the understanding that finding a job *was* my new job, and knowing that there were tools and resources available to help. I had a date for my classes and realized that Jean wouldn't be letting me slack off in the process. I figured out that Jean was going to point me towards the resources, guide me in the process, and then stand back and let me make my way through this by myself.

I discovered what was wrong with my resume. I learned to develop "elevator speeches." We talked about industry choices. Networking. I defined my career goals.

I kept a log of where I had applied, with copies of the resume and cover letter that went with the application. (I eventually learned to keep a copy of the job description as well, because the same job was often posted by different agencies and double applications were disqualified.) Following up on the applications was quite difficult as I rarely had a contact name, let alone a phone number or other contact information.

I was still hollow, though. I had been shaken to the core and felt pretty worthless. Gradually, though, through my weekly chats with Jean, I started to separate my view of myself from my view of my work. Somewhere along the line I suggested to Jean that my layoff was more like a divorce—after 24 ½ years, what else could it be? Like a spurned spouse, I had to redefine myself in terms of myself, not as part of that "couple." Besides, that company was paying "alimony," and it naturally followed that Jean became my "divorce counselor."

Once I could start to see that it was "them" and not "me," I started to heal. I went off for a week of training and obtained the certification that was missing from my resume. I had the skills and plenty of experience, just not that piece of paper. I updated my resume and continued sending out applications.

I have never been comfortable with networking. I hate asking for things and don't want to use my friends. Again, Jean was there with an observation: "How do you feel when a friend asks you for help?" and "Why aren't you letting them have that good feeling of being able to help you?" Ah, such wisdom!

I learned to network—at least in the virtual space. I used LinkedIn to find out more about some of the jobs I applied for and whether I had connections in various companies. I talked to friends and to friends of friends. I discovered Vistaprint.com and had personal business cards made. I refined my elevator speech and actually gave it once in an elevator.

Our weekly team sessions were an opportunity to cheer one another on and to celebrate when a new friend landed a new job. I liked having to be accountable for the hours I was spending and the effort I was putting forth, and I gradually realized that I could have a life beyond the job search. I went out and weeded the flowerbeds. And then it finally happened!

After about three months of sending out resumes and applications, I started to get replies! Oh, happy day! I started to average several phone screens a week. I learned more about the process and answered their questions:

- My long tenure with one company was viewed as a risk: Can you adapt?
- I was applying for contractor positions: Can you adjust?
- The jobs were in Philadelphia: Can you commute?

Then some of those turned into interviews. Finally, the wonderful call came: "Can you start next week?" A small contracting firm had decided to take a chance on presenting me to one of their major clients, and my interview had gone well. I hadn't gotten home from Philadelphia after that interview when I got the call that the hiring paperwork package was being FedExed to my house. Finally! It was my turn to bring the goodies to the team meeting and celebrate *my* landing.

All seemed to be right in the world again, and it continued to be for nearly two years. I converted from contractor to employee for that client at about the one-year mark, and things were looking pretty good. Right before I left on a vacation, my boss and I discussed the possibility that I might work from home a bit more often, and maybe travel to Washington more frequently.

We got back from vacation late Monday, and I spent the day on Tuesday with laundry and the like. I went into the office on Wednesday and was surprised to learn that our consultants were gone. Their contract had ended on the preceding Friday. I started to hear little voices in my head, and most of them were saying things I cannot repeat. I watched as my peers went downstairs to the program director's office in seniority order, one each half-hour. I went downstairs at 9:30, knowing what was waiting for me down there.

Yep. The program director and the HR representative. The misspelled severance folder. I had the presence of mind to point that out, and say, "You must have meant to call someone else—that's not my last name!" The HR person apologized and we started through the papers. He was inordinately nervous, so I tried to make him feel more at ease. "Oh, that's the 'you're not being discriminated against because of your age' paper. We don't need to spend time on that."

Knowing what to expect made it so much easier this time! They gave me a business card for the outplacement agency that had been chosen for us. Because the bulk of the layoffs were occurring at headquarters, and because our location was going to be closed, the outplacement agency was located some 300 miles away. We would have access to them by phone only. Oh, how convenient!

I went back up to my office and found my friends standing there in shock. One colleague named Colin had flown in from the Midwest just for this "meeting," and had already changed his flight back home—but it wouldn't leave until the next morning. I told Kathy to meet me at my house, and that I was taking Colin home with me. We would spend some time filling those hours so that he wasn't alone. And so we left the office.

Over the next few hours, the three of us sat in my living room eating freshly baked chocolate chip cookies (sainthood for the inventor of slice-n-bake cookies!) and rehashing our former employment. When my husband got home, he found us sprawled about laughing about something, cookie crumbs everywhere, and one of the dogs with his nose in a glass of milk. Because dinner seemed to be the appropriate thing, we went off to get a pizza, and then to take Colin back to his hotel. On the way, we decided to stop by our old office (they hadn't taken our badges—we were to mail them to headquarters). We trouped up to the office and calmly removed our personal effects, chuckling that we would love to be a fly on the wall the next day when our boss came in and discovered our stuff gone.

The next morning found me again at my computer. I dug out my old spreadsheet for tracking my applications, updated the resume, and started to look at the job postings.

It's important to note here that I wasn't starting from zero this time. I had my resume, and it had last been updated about two months earlier. I knew to save it in multiple formats. I had a basic cover letter that I had finally gotten into good shape from the first time around, and I had a system for saving the descriptions, cover letters, resume, and all in a series of folders. I had a decent network in place. Moreover, and most important, I knew that I was the same person with the same skills and value on that Thursday as I had been on Monday. It had taken me a while to learn that the first time, but I already knew it this time. I knew that I would find the right position because I had skills and experience to bring to my next employer. This wasn't a divorce; we had just been living together and "he lost his lease and was moving back home" to headquarters.

I did follow some of the same patterns as before: I checked the job listings daily. I discovered the current job description keywords, and I went off to get another certification. I also did some things very differently: I allowed myself more time for myself, again weeding the garden, but also taking the dogs for long walks and meeting my sister for lunch. I was still spending about the same amount of time on the search, but I had learned how to read job descriptions better. I knew how to spot the duplicate listings. I had the basic letters written and could tailor them with relative ease for the particular position in the listing. I knew my list of wants, and further could discern the must-haves from the nice-to-haves. I had a relatively clear picture of my skills and the words that would be used to select for those skills in the job descriptions.

As I applied and got responses, I asked if I could add that person to my professional network. I explained that if someone in my network would be a good fit for their organization, I would be in touch. Most said yes. I followed up with e-mail thank-you notes, complete with links to my LinkedIn profile and my personal, professional Web site. I had built that electronic resume before an interview with an online marketing company, to show that my use of technology was current. While I didn't get that position, I ended up with a nice marketing tool and added it to my personal business cards.

I read job postings and passed them along to Kathy and Colin. Colin landed within a month and tried to recruit me for another position in his company. Kathy and I had long talks, and I read and reread her resume as she polished it. We talked about expectations and what we wanted out of our next positions. We practiced interviews with each other and celebrated when she landed her new job. While I was the last of our little threesome to land, when I did, I had found what I wanted, complete with a decent commute and a higher salary than I had had before—even more amazing because I landed in November 2009, just as things turned bad in both our economy and the job market.

I still check the job listings periodically, and my job board robots still drop matches into my inbox. I have landed, but I'm not complacent. My resume is relatively current, although I need to update my Web site. My LinkedIn profile is up to date, and my network continues to grow. When a recruiter calls and asks if I'm looking, my answer is "I'm never 'not looking.'" There is always a chance that things could change where I'm working, or I may decide that I want something different. Another friend may benefit from a networking contact that I make this week. The world of employment is just too unstable to take for granted anymore.

By Diane McHutchison, PMP, SSBB
Senior Project Manager, Specialty Care

PART 2

MYTHS, LIES, AND OTHER OBSTACLES

CHAPTER 13

LIE: I'LL GET THE FIRST JOB I APPLY FOR

Rejection is not a lot of fun. Most of us do whatever we can to avoid it because it hurts, brings us down, and makes a trip to the dentist feel like a vacation. Rejection, especially a lot of it, can make people wonder about themselves—so that when they look at their own resumes or talk about their backgrounds, they have the feeling that they're lying. They couldn't possibly have been successful in the past if this company or individual is turning them down now for a position that's a perfect match. And of course this stirs up the ultimate rejection: being downsized or let go.

Rejection can also make you wonder about cause and effect. It's reasonable to believe that if you do a good job at an interview, or send your resume off in response to a posting that sounds as if it's written for your exact qualifications, that you'll get a positive reaction. But many times what happens is nothing (and this is in some ways the most difficult to process), or you're turned down. If you're not prepared for this inevitable part of the job search process, it can be devastating.

So first of all, it's helpful to understand the job search process and then create ways to prepare for rejection and other odd phenomena. It's a little like getting ready for battle: You've got to be in shape and you need the right armor.

Why is this process so strange? If you haven't had to look for a job in a while, it might feel strange and frustrating because it's an unknown. It's foreign territory. It's different now than when you looked for a job 10 years ago. And some of this is positive: The power of the Internet is a huge help in finding information, researching companies, and making your background visible. But other aspects aren't so user friendly:

- You apply online and don't hear a thing.
- Recruiters call you saying that you're the perfect fit for an executive position that they're handling, and then they never call you back.
- A company invites you in for an interview and then changes its mind. Or worse, you get there only to discover that the interviewer is unprepared and isn't really hiring.

This is where you need to tell yourself that right now you have a steep learning curve. You've got to find out, through your own experience and others', what's realistic to expect. As one very clever client of mine said, "Hope for short; prepare for long." And of course, you have to adapt your techniques to the market, especially in a tough economy.

I urge my clients to run a balanced search and to go after the unpublished job market as well as the published one. So it's smart to post your resume on key sites, answer online ads, and work with recruiters. But if your focus is entirely on the published side of the market (meaning that all your competition is going after the same leads), you're likely in for a long and difficult search—despite the fact that the Internet makes you feel productive. To be effective, you need to be proactive, and that can include

- Coming up with a list of companies that make sense to pursue given your background.
- Learning how to network effectively (and this might include building your LinkedIn connections and other social media presence).
- Figuring out the best ways to get through to hiring managers because they're the ones who can make the decision to bring you on board.

These are critical issues to monitor. It's really easy to get sucked into the Internet postings and then wonder why nothing is happening. As you create your search schedule, include all these ways of looking for work so that you shorten your search and get past the rejections faster.

When I tell my clients that rejection is the sign of a healthy search, I can see disbelief and suspicion on their faces. They begin to wonder whether I'm off the deep end. So I do my best to explain that this is a process in which no one, no matter what their qualifications are, bats one thousand. It just doesn't happen. As you begin your job search campaign, tell yourself that you will get a bunch of *no's*, some *maybes*, some *almosts*, and then finally a *yes*—or more than one *yes*. This is a reasonable expectation, whereas thinking that everyone is going to love you and offer you twice the money you were making before is not.

Let's go back to the "in shape and right armor" concept. In shape might mean that you're comfortable with your verbal communications regarding why you were let go, what you're looking for, and specific examples that prove your accomplishments. It could also include, as explained previously, running a well-balanced search and getting advice from others so that you're not limited to your own point of view. And the armor might mean balancing your search with other activities that you enjoy (sports, exercise, volunteering, baking, and so on), helping others who are also looking for work, joining professional associations (because this keeps you up to date and involved in your function and/or industry), and learning to expect rejection. It's a huge mistake to give others the power to define you, so if a company isn't smart enough to hire you, it's their loss. But, of course, you need to learn from the *no's* so that each time you interview, you get better at it.

A note here on perfection: It's easy to idealize your last job because everything looks better than the process of looking for work. But it's important to remember that your past position wasn't perfect and your new one won't be, either. It's a job, not a magic wand. It will have aspects you really enjoy and others that frustrate you. That's just the way it is. I think this realization also helps in handling rejection.

THAT DOESN'T MAKE SENSE!

Fred was in sales. He was really good at his work and had grown professionally in his industry: sportswear. He saw the writing on the wall and was prepared for job loss. Within a week of losing his job, he had his resume completed and was actively posting it, responding to ads, and networking.

Because he was in a niche industry, word got around, but he was smart and made sure that the message about himself was positive. Instead of "poor Fred," he told people what had happened at his former company and made sure they understood that being let go was not a performance issue. He also communicated that he was excited to be looking for a new opportunity where he could use his extensive knowledge of the sportswear market to help a company maximize its sales.

At the end of the first month of his search, he had an interview with his top company. He loved its product line, and the territory was convenient and close to home. Plus someone he knew was connected to the person who would be his boss and was happy to put in a good word for him.

Fred practiced his accomplishment stories: what he'd done in his past jobs, including quantifiable results. He did really well at the interview and told me that he thought this was "in the bag." A week later there was no word and HR hadn't asked for references. He e-mailed the hiring manager and got a response that said, "You're still a top candidate but we're also interviewing a few other people." Fred called me and wondered if this was just a formality because he knew he was the perfect fit. My advice was to keep moving: Find new companies to pursue and keep networking as if this opportunity won't work out.

"That doesn't make sense," he said.

"You're right," I told him, "but this is a tricky process and there are many unknowns, so it's smart to act as if you don't have this job until proven otherwise."

"But why should I do all that work when I know this job is mine?"

"Can you imagine how hard it would be to crank your search back up to high gear when you've basically let it come to a halt because you hoped you were getting an offer? This is where rejection really gets to you, so my advice would be to keep going and keep a good portion of your efforts in new leads."

(continued)

(continued)

He agreed, and two weeks later he found out that he wasn't chosen. It hurt and it was discouraging, but he was prepared and was actively pursuing other competitors. His next interview went really well. Again, he had people from his network who put in a good word for him and also gave him inside information about the company that helped him address their needs at the interview. He received an offer shortly after that, negotiated the salary, and started his new job. Fred learned that the best way to protect himself from rejection was to keep moving and keep his search active, even after a great interview when it didn't seem to make sense to keep searching.

Quick Do's and Don'ts

Do:

1. Think about how you can get in shape so that you're prepared for rejection. Sharing your goals and expectations with others can help.

2. Practice your accomplishment stories so that it's easy for you to prove the specific ways you've made a difference in the past. I always ask my clients to be ready to answer the "Why should I hire you?" question.

3. Balance your search in two critical ways: Go after the unpublished jobs as well as those that are advertised, and make sure you're putting time and energy into other activities that could expand your market. This might include gaining a new certification, updating your skills, or researching industries related to your most recent one.

Don't:

1. Expect to get the first job you apply for or interview for. (This lie or wildly optimistic expectation is a setup for disappointment.)

2. Hope for excellent communications or feedback from hiring managers, human resource professionals, or recruiters. These are busy people, and many times you'll have to remind yourself that "no news is no news." This means that not hearing anything doesn't necessarily mean one thing or another.

3. Let the rejection that is an inherent part of this process bring you down. Okay, you can let it bother you for a short while, but then get back to work.

Resources and Ideas

In chapter 1 we looked at ways to get past the initial shock of job loss. Some of these suggestions may also help you process the rejection you're experiencing:

- Ask for feedback when you've been rejected for a position, so that you gain information that might help you do better in the future. One client was told that she "wasn't enthusiastic enough." This was an easy fix. Using a video camera, I taped her answering interview questions and made sure that her body language (posture, facial expressions, and gestures) conveyed energy and enthusiasm.

- Figure out what you need to be able to stay proactive and motivated. You might need to take a little time off to recharge your batteries. Or some affirmation might help: In some of the workshops I teach, I have the participants introduce each other. It can be really inspiring and motivating to hear someone else talk about your background and accomplishments.

- Analyze what you might do differently. Do you need to adjust your daily schedule? Is your search map getting you to companies that might hire you? Where are you getting traction? That might be an area to focus on.

- Introduce yourself with enthusiasm and don't start by explaining why you're no longer with your former company. That's a sad message and doesn't motivate others to help you. Hearing your own positive message will also help you counter the inevitable rejection that's part of finding a new position.

CHAPTER 14

OBSTACLE: I DON'T HAVE ENOUGH EDUCATION (OR I HAVE TOO MUCH)

In my experience, there are two components of the educational challenge: no college degree or too many. Let's look at both of these to see how you might handle them if your situation is similar.

Having no degree is the situation I encounter more frequently, and this is why: A person gets a good job right out of high school. It may be that his family can't afford to send him to college. Then he gets promoted, receives excellent training as well as an on-the-job education, and does really well. He thinks about going to school at night to get a college degree, but often his life is complicated by other responsibilities and he doesn't have time—or doesn't make time. This didn't pose a problem at work; however, now that he's thrown into the job market, he's terrified that no one will hire him because he doesn't have a college degree. And to make it worse, many ads include the phrase "college degree required."

Like your statement about why you were let go, this is one that also needs preparation and practice. You want to be honest but also strategic, meaning you're going to put the most positive spin on this that you can. So here's an example:

> *When I graduated from high school, I became really interested in manufacturing and was lucky enough to be hired by a leading maker of consumer goods. The company had an excellent training program and I took every course I could. This helped me get promoted regularly, and while I wanted to get my college degree, the demands of work didn't make that a practical option. If you talk to my references, they'll tell you that I'm the type of manager who is always one step ahead of a challenge. Once I understand a problem, I make sure I have the skills to solve it.*

So the implied message here is, "I don't have my degree, but that hasn't gotten in my way. I'm effective without it." Obviously, the way you say this is critically important. We believe what we see and hear—not just the words. Don't memorize a script, but say your statement enough times that you're comfortable with it and can deliver it with confidence.

Another part of your message could be that you'd be very happy to get your degree now (and if you're lucky, the company might have a tuition-reimbursement program). Or, you can mention that you've just gained a new certification or other credential that keeps you current in your field. This is why joining and attending professional associations is so critical: You find out what others in your field are doing and stay up to date with what's in demand.

When you see ads that require a college degree, my advice would be to respond to them if you're a good fit with the rest of the requirements. This means you match at least 85 to 90 percent of what they're looking for. Some companies stick to the college degree requirement and others don't. You don't have anything to lose by sending in an application; and if you can find someone within that company to help promote your candidacy, your chances increase dramatically.

So now for the opposite problem: too many degrees. The highly educated job seeker might threaten less-educated hiring managers and might also face a salary challenge— that his or her compensation is too high. The best way to address the salary issue that may be associated with advanced degrees is to state clearly why you're interested in a particular position and to defer the compensation question as long as possible. The reason you want to put off this conversation is that the more they want you, the better chance you'll have of getting a good offer. If you sense that someone at the company you're exploring is nervous about this, you can tell him or her that you're confident you can reach an agreement that's fair to both parties. You could also add that you'll be glad to share your full salary history at the appropriate time. If push comes to shove and the interviewer asks you point blank, "What were you making?" you can tell him or her your past compensation but state that your current salary requirements are flexible. This is a polite way of saying, "Salary isn't the most critical issue and I'd really rather not talk about this just yet."

In the situation where you have a higher degree or other credentials that are superior to the person you would be reporting to, the best you can do is watch your demeanor so that in the interview process, the hiring manager sees that you are interested in his or her opinion, that you have an open mind, and that you're not out to take over his or her job. Asking questions is a great way to do this because it conveys both interest and respect and demonstrates your collaborative style.

Another challenge job seekers with advanced degrees face is that their market may be shrinking. I work with a fair number of research scientists, mostly Ph.D.s, whose work has been outsourced to other countries. So although they're highly qualified, their degrees don't guarantee them an easy time of finding another research position. If you think of the quantity of jobs forming a pyramid, there are a lot more junior-level jobs than there are senior ones. So as you advance, you're moving up into the level where there are fewer jobs. My CEO, CFO, and COO clients know that their search may take close to a year because of the limited opportunities.

Education is an important credential, so for my clients with MBAs, Ph.D.s, or MDs, I make sure these degrees stand out on page one of their resumes. And the same is true for key certifications such as being a Six Sigma Black Belt or Certified Project Manager. I'm currently working with an M.D. who has a fantastic background in compliance. One of the challenges that we're working on together is how he can avoid threatening the people who are interviewing him. This is a rare occurrence, but my advice to him has been to make his listening skills his top priority, and to be careful not to overwhelm the interviewers with more information than they need.

So whether you have no college degree or have several advanced degrees, build your search strategy around who you are and what you have to offer. Don't let the lack of a degree stop you: There are plenty of smart and highly successful people without them. In both cases (many degrees or none), you still face the same challenge of selling yourself effectively. Make a list of your key accomplishments and, in your written and verbal communications, be sure to highlight how you've made a difference, whether your role was administrative or top management. Your work history—specifically your accomplishments—provides proof to others of what you've done and what you can do for them.

DO DEGREES MATTER?

The first CEO client I worked with had no college degree. After high school he joined the army; and right out of the military he began his career in the insurance industry. Within a short time he worked his way up to a management position, and then on to senior management, and finally CEO. His company went through some tough times, and the board decided to let him go. As we worked on his resume together, we made sure to include both the courses he had attended and his certifications. It was obvious from his background that he knew his industry and was a strong leader. What really helped—in addition to a positive attitude— was that he had an extensive network of senior-level contacts. These contacts got him around the hiring bureaucracy where his lack of a degree might have disqualified him. He was also comfortable with his own background and was able to prove how he had been effective in the past. This winning combination helped him land a new CEO position in less than a year.

A recent client who had the opposite problem was a research scientist with a Ph.D. in biology. After 22 years with a major pharmaceutical firm, he found himself in the job market. After trying to find another position with a pharmaceutical firm, he followed the suggestion of a friend and pursued an academic position at a local college. Not only did this process drag on for months, but it also required a lot of effort in providing the specific documents that they required, all for a potential job that would have paid about half his former salary. After many months, he was told that they had chosen someone else. So although he had the degrees they wanted, the college was more comfortable selecting a candidate who had spent his career in academia, not industry.

Once he recovered from this setback, he added biotech companies to his search goals and was hired for a prospecting position with a company developing its U.S. market. Although it wasn't a perfect fit for him (because he would be doing more sales than science), he realized that he would gain tremendous exposure to other companies through this role. So he saw it as a way to get through a tough job market and make contacts that could lead to a better job. The point here is that even with an advanced degree, he ran into obstacles and had to find the market that was expanding and would hire him.

Quick Do's and Don'ts

Do:

1. Figure out your educational communication strategy and get comfortable explaining it to others.

2. Decide whether you need to invest in additional training. Check with your local One-Stop Career Center to see whether there are funds to help with this.

3. Ask about other resources for enhancing your education. Where I live, the local community college offers free tuition for up to 30 credits to unemployed residents.

4. Do everything you can to stay current in your field. This could include reading trade journals and blogs, attending conferences, and joining professional associations.

Don't:

1. Assume you can't get a job because you don't have a degree or have too many.

2. Apologize for your past. It is what it is and you need to show how you've been effective no matter what your educational credentials are.

3. Think that a college degree is a magic wand. It's not. I'm sure you know people who have degrees who aren't particularly good at what they do. It's wonderful to have a good education, but it's not the only ticket to being a strong contributor.

Resources and Ideas

Here are some ideas for overcoming education-related obstacles:

- Whenever you experience an obstacle in your search, it's smart to get ideas from others. In the outplacement industry where I work, I think we sometimes drive our clients a bit crazy by harping on the importance of networking. But to use a cliché, two heads really are better than one. You don't have to think of it as networking, but instead as having a board or advisory panel to whom you can turn when you're stuck or need advice.

- Networking is particularly important if you're changing careers, targeting a new industry, have an educational issue, or are creating your own company. How you might ask someone to help you could go like this: "As you know, I left XYZ Company and am excited to be expanding my search for a new [fill in the blank] position in [the new industry], as well as in the one where I've worked. If you have time, I'd like to get your advice as I create and implement my search strategy. This wouldn't be a time-intensive commitment, but once a month I'd like to check in with you—maybe for 15 minutes over the phone—or occasionally send you documents or meet in person. Is that something you'd feel comfortable doing?" (You could also add, before asking this last question, why that person's perspective would be particularly helpful.)

- Don't forget the reference librarian at your local library. These people are smart and know how to find information. It's an interesting thing that most of us really enjoy solving other people's problems (which always seem easier to work out than our own). Tap into this and your search will flourish.

- Lastly, you're never too old to go back to school if that is something you want to do and can afford. I've worked with clients of all ages who are thrilled to be students again and often end up being mentors to the younger students in the class. Community colleges offer work-related courses at a reasonable rate, and some colleges offer credit for work experience.

CHAPTER 15

MYTH: I'M TOO OLD TO GET A JOB

I'd like to say that if I had a nickel for every time I've heard this particular myth, I'd be a wealthy woman indeed. Not to be unsympathetic, but there are many examples of highly effective people working well into their 70s and 80s, so when I hear this from someone who is barely 50, I wonder what's really going on. The sad truth is that many of the clients I work with really believe that their age is the reason they'll never work again, and so they give up before they even try to run an effective job search campaign.

Here's my lecture—what I share with the people I like to call my "mature" clients (and being no spring chicken myself, I feel qualified to talk about this age group). The facts:

- Will a company hire younger workers more readily than older ones? Sometimes.

- Will age be seen as a problem? That depends both on how you come across and how well you fit the company's needs.

- Do younger workers have advantages? Yes, they're cheaper and more malleable.

- Do older workers have the advantage of experience and stability? Yes.

- Do many older workers have a better work ethic than younger ones? Yes.

- Are mature workers a lot less likely to be out on maternity or paternity leave? For sure!

- Will many hiring managers realize that if their teams or divisions are made up entirely of younger workers, they'll have some serious problems? Yes.

- Is being up to date in your field critical, especially as an older worker? Yes.

- If you're older and you're turned down for a position, is it age discrimination? Hard to tell.

- Do your nonverbal communications and overall image become increasingly important if you're older? Absolutely.

Okay, so you get the picture. It's not simple. Here's an example from a client I was working with recently. I don't know her age, but my guess is she was in her mid-50s. Her background was in administration, customer service, and sales support. She was good at what she did and had a reputation as an excellent problem solver. She started her program with me a few months ago. We completed her resume and some other aspects of her search foundation and then she disappeared. After a few weeks and a number of attempts on my part, she agreed to meet with me again. I asked her, "How's it going?"

She was slumped in the chair and leaned her head on her hand. "Terrible."

When I asked for details, she told me that she had applied to a ton of positions but hadn't had one nibble. One of her goals was to work for the military or the government, and the application process for this market was daunting. She told me of the hours she spent filling in online applications. Her conclusion to all this: "I'm too old. No one will hire me."

So, first of all, I asked her how anyone reading her resume would know her age. Yes, her work history went back to the mid-80s, but if she started work at 18, and had worked for approximately 24 years, that would make her only 42. (In resume writing, we tend to focus on the most recent 15 years of employment and then summarize early experience, often leaving out the early dates. For mature workers with degrees, we again can delete the graduation dates. This isn't lying; it's simply strategic.)

She couldn't answer this question. Then I asked her if she had registered with employment agencies, because this is often a quick way for someone with an administrative background to find temporary work. I took out the local phone book, turned to the Yellow Pages, and showed her some listings under "Employment Agencies." She could see that several of these placed people in customer service as well as in administrative roles. So I suggested she contact them and be prepared for both interviews and a test of her skills.

Her objection here was that she didn't want a temporary job, so I explained that many of these positions become permanent but that it's an easier way to get hired because the company can "try before they buy." It also was a way for her to keep her options open because both the agency and the company where she would be temping expected her to keep her job search active.

"What a great position to be in," I told her, "to be working, expanding your network, getting paid, and then have some really neat bargaining power because you have an offer from another company. If you really like your temp position and they have the budget to make you permanent, this can be the outcome."

She looked at me as if I were speaking another language. I saw in her face that she still believed that this was just talk and that no one would hire her because she was too old. I took a deep breath and asked her to please tell me what she's good at. She did this. Then I asked her if she still had those skills or if she'd lost them.

"What?" she asked.

"Can you still do the things you just described to me?"

"Of course."

"Okay. So if a company hired you, you could help with their administrative tasks, customer service, or sales support. Right?"

She nodded. And then I explained the three components of age as I see it: chronological age, skill set, and the impression you make. I told her that she couldn't do anything about how old she was. (This was the first thing I said that she agreed with.) But before letting her wallow in this for long, I added that she could do something about the other two.

Because we'd already talked about her skill set (and she was up to date in her field), we moved on to the last factor: how she came across. I explained that the impression we make on others is highly visual and can be influenced by clothing, hairstyle, makeup, and more (these are not my areas of expertise, but I suggested that she get help from someone if she wanted feedback). The impression is also influenced by body language: posture; facial expression; eye contact; handshake; gestures; and vocal issues such as volume, inflection, and pace. And in these areas I could help her by videotaping a mock interview and then reviewing it with her.

For the older or mature worker, I told her, it's particularly important to make a positive impression. We can't risk that potential employers see us as tired and worn out, coasting, or just interested in a paycheck. They must see that we love our work and are good at it—that we're fired up. The way each of us conveys this will be different and that's just fine. But it's not optional—we must show that we're "young at heart" as the Frank Sinatra song goes. (Now I'm really dating myself.)

She left my office promising to change her search methods and to work on how she came across. I've got my fingers crossed.

DON'T GROAN WHEN YOU SIT DOWN

Here's my favorite job search story as it relates to age. Ed was a 65-year-old process engineer. He had worked for one pharmaceutical company for his entire career. He loved his work and was devastated by losing his job. As I got to know him, we discovered that we both loved tennis. He played more frequently than I did. At one of our sessions, as he sat down at the table where we met, he let out a groan.

"Hey, Ed," I said. "What was that?"

"What was what?"

"That noise you made when you sat down."

"Oh," he said, laughing, "I played an extra set of doubles last night and my knees are killing me."

(continued)

(continued)

"Out you go," I said.

"What?"

"Could you please come into my office again and sit down without groaning, even if it hurts?"

"Boy, you're tough," he said, getting carefully out of his chair.

He humored me and came back in, sitting down with no signs of discomfort.

"Well done," I told him. Then we talked about why this was so important. He got it—he knew it was critical to come across as fit and with it. He wasn't trying to hide his age and he wasn't embarrassed by it, but what he wanted to project, what he hoped others perceived, was that he was a strong contributor, that he knew his stuff, and that age was not an issue.

Ed did something else that many of my clients won't do: He went on an interview no matter where it was located. At the very least, he figured, it was practice. His thinking was that he didn't have to worry about the location until he had an offer. So he interviewed in the Midwest, in New England, and eventually close by in New Jersey. He got an offer from the local company and accepted it. A year later he e-mailed me to tell me that he had found a better job with another company and had taken that. He was 66 and enjoying himself. And he didn't groan when he sat down in a chair!

Quick Do's and Don'ts

Do:

1. Plan your strategy to deal with age issues. (This could also include the more rare issue—you're too young—or you look a lot younger than your real age.)

2. Get comfortable with your answers related to age questions such as "Why should I hire you?" "When do you plan to retire?" and so on.

3. Get feedback on your appearance from a source you trust—but not someone you live with.

4. Make a list of people you admire who are close to your age and see what it is about them that you like.

Don't:

1. Decide before you've even started your search that age has knocked you out of the job market.

2. Complain. This is one of the fastest ways to make others think you're old and cranky.

3. Talk about your health or lack of it. Again, this is not motivating to others.

4. Groan when you sit down in a chair. Interviewing is an athletic process and you need to show you're fit. (If you have a disability, that's another issue. Like other possible obstacles, you have to find a way to talk about it.)

Resources and Ideas

I think one of the most difficult things for many of us is to admit we need help and to get our minds turned around so that we don't see this as a weakness or failure. Why should you automatically be able to run an effective job search campaign? How could you possibly know ways to get through the ups and downs of job loss if this is the first time it has happened to you? And when your search is complicated by the age issue, this connecting with others and getting opinions from diverse sources isn't optional—it's critical.

If you're concerned about your age, here are some questions that might be helpful as you network:

- How do I come across? Do you have any suggestions for improvement?
- What do you see as my main selling point?
- Should I include on my resume that I'm a black belt in tae kwon do? (Yes!)
- What companies do you think might be particularly interested in my depth of experience?
- Should I consider consulting? Who do you know who might be willing to talk to me about that?
- Would you look at my list of companies and share with me what you know about them? (This is smart because you're using networking to get around a possible obstacle.)
- Should I start working out? (If your doctor says it's fine, that's a great idea.)
- Do you have time to listen to my top accomplishment stories and to give me feedback on them?

CHAPTER 16

MYTH: I DON'T HAVE A NETWORK (AND NETWORKING IS CREEPY, ANYWAY)

This aversion to networking is one that I hear quite often. Faced with job loss, people who have numerous and diverse contacts suddenly decide that they don't know anyone. They've grown up in a bubble and live in a cabin in the woods where they grow their own food. You get the picture. I nod and smile, and when they're finished telling me this sad story, I launch into my networking speech.

The first thing we often talk about is what networking isn't. It's not cold calling. It's not imposing on people. It's not feeling wildly uncomfortable (although for most of us, there is a hump of discomfort to get over as we learn a new skill or improve one we forgot we had).

"You do have to be a salesperson of sorts in this endeavor, but you're not making a list of people and then calling them to see if they have a job for you," I say.

At this point there is sometimes a glimmer of relief from my clients. But more often, they sit there, looking at me with a blank expression. If they're really resistant to this part of the process, they may ask

> *I don't see why you people in outplacement harp on this so much. I got my last job through an ad in the paper. Why do I have to do this and how can you say that most jobs are found this way?*

My first answer to this is to explain that we (career professionals) don't know how you're going to get your next job. And we also don't know how long your search will take. But what we do know is what makes an effective search, because we understand the hiring process. Being part of hundreds of searches every year, we learn a lot and see what works. And yes we throw statistics around about the percentage of jobs that are found through networking (this is in the 75 percent range), but rather than worry about this, I think it's a good idea to focus on two things:

1. How do you get recommendations if you're going to buy a product, such as a new car or a new roof?
2. What is the most effective way to get to decision makers so that you can beat out the competition?

As we discuss the first issue, what often surfaces is that it's not so hard to ask others about their roofer. But when it's a job search and you're the product, it's creepy. This kind of focus on ourselves feels awkward and weird. My thoughts here are that this is exactly right; most of us aren't used to promoting ourselves. At work we focus on what we have to get done, and except for performance reviews, we don't turn the microscope on ourselves. In job search, as awkward as this may feel, you have to do it. You must be able to talk about what you're good at and how you've made a difference.

In your written materials (resume, cover e-mails, job applications, and so on), you want to show your accomplishments. And as you prepare your verbal communications, whether for networking or interviewing, you need to be able to talk about yourself with precision and enthusiasm. "This is what I did and here's how it made a difference" is your basic template. Practice these statements talking to the dog, your neighbors, and your search buddies. But don't memorize them as a canned script; otherwise, you'll sound stiff and rehearsed, and when you're nervous you'll go blank.

So on to the second issue: What is the most effective way to get to decision makers so that you can beat out the competition? I'm a great proponent of what I like to call the combo method. This means that you go after opportunities using more than one technique. Let's say you see an ad and it's perfect—it was written for you. You answer it, but then instead of going nuts waiting for the phone to ring, you see whether you can find someone who works for that company (assuming that the ad gives the company's name). Through your network—that is, the people you know from work or outside activities, your family, school or college friends, and so on—you reach out with a simple message:

> *I've found an interesting opportunity at XYZ company and I'm trying to find someone who works there so that I can connect with the decision maker. Do you know anyone there?*

As in all networking, if you sense resistance, explain that you aren't asking for a personal recommendation, but with an inside contact you'll have a much better chance both of understanding whether this is a good fit and of being in the candidate pool brought in for interviews. If there is still hesitation, this would be a good time to prove why your background might be exactly what they need (by giving an accomplishment story that shows you've done your homework).

Critically important in networking is that your message is positive. This isn't the time or place to tell others how bad the market is and that "no one is hiring." Negative messages turn people off. And it's not a guilt trip where the implied message might be, "You have a job and I don't, so you owe me a favor." You're sharing your goals or mission statement and then asking for help (this could be general information or a referral). At Lee Hecht Harrison we urge our clients to have a list of companies that they're targeting and to use this as a key networking tool. The reason this is effective is that it's proactive and it motivates others to help you because you've done the groundwork. (See appendix C for how to put this together.)

As you lay the foundation for your job search, make a list of the people you know. Look at this list several times a day and add to it. Don't filter people out, thinking, "Oh, they'd never help me" or "I can't contact him because we lost touch 20 years ago." A scientist on the team I facilitate shared recently that he'd been connecting with former college friends and that the response had been wonderful. He was afraid that because he'd been out of contact so long, they would think, "Oh, he's only connecting with me now because he's lost his job." But because his message was upbeat and positive, the opposite was true. These former friends were thrilled to hear from him and were happy to help.

FRICK AND FRACK

Here are two stories, bookends if you will, that illustrate the two extremes of networking. Joan was in IT. She had been regularly promoted and she was technically up to date. She'd been with her former company for 18 years and hadn't had to think about looking for work, networking, or keeping her resume current. She was stunned by job loss; and after several weeks, she didn't feel any better. She was angry and resentful and it showed. She joined my weekly team and brought in her report (we track certain data to help clients maintain high productivity). On the part of the chart that showed contacts, all categories were blank. She wasn't talking to anyone.

As we discussed issues of concern from the team members, networking often came up. She sat there with a stony look on her face. Finally she said, "I don't know how to do it and I'm not sure I want to do it." Other team members shared their experience in learning how to network and why they thought it was valuable. Another month went by and she was unchanged. I talked to her privately and offered help and additional resources. Her response was that she had decided to drop off the team. She didn't see any point in trying.

Art began the search process with an open attitude. He wasn't sure what to do, but he was willing to explore suggestions and to experiment. Like Joan, he had been with his former company for nearly 20 years and hadn't kept his network active. He got his resume done, practiced his verbal communications, and created his target list of companies. He quickly found that this list was a great motivator to others. Before long he had two to three networking meetings a week. He used his list both to get the meeting set up and also as an agenda for the meetings themselves. He told the team that he was really surprised that people would see him, taking time out of their busy schedules. In some cases he took them out for coffee or lunch, and in others he arranged a 30-minute meeting in their offices. He was careful of the time and never went over the agreed-upon amount. At about the four-month mark, in one of these meetings, he learned about a small company in his industry that he'd never heard of. He was referred in through this contact, got an interview, and within a few weeks started his new job.

In this case, not only did networking lead Art to a great opportunity, but it also gave him structure and an industry edge. The meetings took a lot of work to set up, prepare for, and conduct, but they got him out of the house, interacting with others, and they almost always made him feel better. Even if the message from the person he was meeting with was, "I'm not sure how I can help you," Art knew that by meeting and then following up, he had additional people helping him keep his finger on the pulse of the market. He has now been at his new job for almost a year, and although he can't network with the same intensity, it has become part of his professional commitment. And he's also happy to help others who are in transition because he learned what networking did for him and wants to "pay it forward."

Quick Do's and Don'ts

Do:

1. Learn about networking. Talk to others and find out what they've done and what has worked for them. Read a book or two about it. Keep an open mind.

2. Make a list of the people you know and keep adding to it. If you're stuck, share it with someone so that they can help you expand it.

3. Create a networking spreadsheet so that you can easily see your contacts, their phone numbers and e-mail addresses, what you've talked about, whether you've sent them your resume or list of companies, and most critically, when you will follow up.

4. Take baby steps if this is difficult. Find a networking mentor. But do it. Many clients that I've worked with find it helpful to set a quota for the day or the week so that this critical effort can't slip.

Don't:

1. Give up before you start.

2. Assume you know what networking is. As you learn more about what it is and isn't, you'll find your own way through this.

3. Let your discouragement leak into your networking message. It's okay to say, "I'm having a hard time with this," but don't shut down networking with generalizations like "the industry is dead" or "that won't work."

4. Let one or two rude or indifferent people stop you from this process. This is quirky and many people find that the contacts they thought would be helpful aren't, and the ones that they expected nothing from open doors for them.

5. Expect your former coworkers to be instantly comfortable networking with you, especially if they're still working. They may feel guilty that they still have

their jobs. You'll have to show them that you're okay with that. A client I met with recently had phoned her boss at her former company three times with no results. Together we decided that she would try reaching out through e-mail, and then if there still was no response, her best tactic was to move on.

Resources and Ideas

Here are some ways to make networking work for you:

- Find your own style. If you're shy, don't assume you won't be successful in this endeavor. Many times shy networkers are excellent listeners.

- Analyze your strengths in networking. Mine, for example, are that I love meeting with new people and readily express enthusiasm. Yours may be that you know the insurance industry inside and out and are generous in sharing information with others.

- If it's helpful, keep a networking journal so that you can write out your goals, frustrations, and ways you worked through them. Looking back at this journal could help you see that you're making progress.

- Find and attend group meetings, whether they're focused on people in transition or have to do with some other interest such as collecting buttons or cancer research. Set yourself a quota for the number of people you will talk to and exchange business cards with at these meetings. One of my rules when I go to meetings of career professionals is to not sit down until the meeting starts. I put my bag on a chair; and armed with my business cards and a pen, I work the room. At the last meeting I went to I made a great contact by talking with the speaker. (I had noticed that she was standing by herself at the front of the room.)

- Read some books on networking. I've listed several in appendix H, "Suggested Reading," but you may want to ask your network which ones they've found particularly helpful. And maybe you can find resources that are tailored for your function, such as networking for teachers, engineers, or marketing professionals.

- Take advantage of social media, whether LinkedIn, Facebook, Twitter, and so on. These make networking so much easier and really help in expanding your contacts and reconnecting with old friends. You can even use LinkedIn to quickly find contacts at your target companies.

- Lastly, networking may feel a bit artificial at first, but as you get better at this critical process, you may actually come to enjoy it. How bad is it to talk to people who do what you do? How painful is it to share your strengths and goals and ask for advice? I hope your answer is, or soon will be, "Not bad at all."

CHAPTER 17

OBSTACLE: MY PRIDE IS HURT

If someone asked you today to solve a complex mathematical equation or to fly a small plane, you'd laugh—unless, of course, you have skills and experience in these areas. Why, then, when you lose your job for the first time (often after many years of working), do most people assume that they naturally should know how to look for work? I wish I knew the answer to this one.

One engineer I worked with years ago came in for his initial meeting with me, attended a few of our classes, and completed his resume. Then he got stuck—unable to move forward. He slept late, didn't return phone calls, gave up on his search, and became discouraged. He wouldn't admit that he didn't know how to look for a job. Instead he came to the conclusion that he'd never work again. I don't know what happened to him because he dropped out of his program with my company. But my guess is that his attitude created a self-fulfilling prophecy.

So if right now this is all new to you and feels overwhelming, please know that you have a lot of company—that many people faced with sudden job loss are shocked and unsure. Just admitting that this is new to you is a great place to begin because it invites others to help you. The "I'm new to this" message is a good one, unlike "I'll never get hired again, so what's the point?" And running a good job search doesn't require advanced degrees or stunning credentials, but it does call for openness and a willingness to learn. Take small steps, consult with others, keep track of what's working and what isn't, adjust your strategy, and you'll make good progress.

I'm sometimes asked about my success rate (how many of my clients land new jobs). After trying to answer this, I came to the conclusion that I can't. There are too many variables; and of course, some clients land new jobs after their programs are over and they don't let me know about it. So my data is inconclusive. But here are factors that affect how successful job seekers are:

- Previous experience in the job search process
- How up to date they are in their function and industry
- Their attitude
- The economy (and this can be very industry specific)

- Mergers and acquisitions (Is their market expanding or shrinking?)
- Their willingness to commit to a process that requires patience, persistence, courage, and good communication skills

To be one of the success stories, you need four qualities:

- **Patience:** The hiring process is never fast enough, whether it takes a week or many months.
- **Persistence:** Effective follow-up will set you apart from many job seekers, and it gives you the chance to show your determination and professionalism.
- **Courage:** Looking for a job is a little bit like being lost in the woods without a compass. There are days when the frustration of it all brings you down, but you can't let it beat you.
- **Focused communication:** You need to be able to articulate who you are, what you're good at, and your goals. And you have to offer specific proof of your value.

There's a lot you can't control in the job search process, but there are many things you can, including the qualities mentioned in the preceding list. Focus on these, be systematic, keep at it, and you'll land a new job. This is what career counselors see every day: There are ups and downs, high points and low points, events that are logical and ones that aren't. But if you stick with it and learn from the process, you'll be working again.

I'M JUST SO ANGRY!

Charlotte had worked for only two companies in her whole career in the plumbing-supply industry. Her background was in operations and she was good at it. Because of her competence and the fact that she worked for a small company, she became an advisor to the CEO/owner. When he was out, she took over. When key decisions had to be made, she was consulted. She loved her job and couldn't imagine that she'd ever lose it. But then the company hired someone in finance who challenged the way Charlotte did things. She questioned her decisions and spoke negatively about her behind her back. Through this rough patch, Charlotte still believed she was indispensable and didn't worry about losing her job. Then she was called into a meeting with the CEO and HR and was told that they were going to eliminate her position. She argued with them and told them why this wasn't possible. She proved all the ways she was actively contributing, but they didn't change their minds. Instead, they thanked her for her past 20 years of service, explained her severance package and outplacement services, and asked her to leave.

We had our first meeting and she was angry. Really angry. Something was wrong and she decided that the new woman had set her up. I cautioned her to be careful because it's often impossible to know what really is behind job loss. She ignored me and ranted about how ungrateful and stupid her former company was. I tried to reason with her and to reassure her that this most likely had nothing to do with her work. She wouldn't agree but finally said she would begin putting her resume together.

Our next meeting wasn't a whole lot more productive because she had found on her former company's Web site a posting for her job. "They lied to me!" she said. "My job wasn't eliminated; they just wanted to get rid of me." I'm never given any background on why a client was let go and I told her that. This made her angrier because she wanted me to agree with her explanation.

By our third meeting, we made a little progress. We got the resume completed and talked about companies that might be of interest to her. She lit up at the thought of working for her former company's competition. She wasn't bound by a noncompete agreement, and so she was free to include whomever she wanted in her list of companies. I asked her not to contact them yet because I was concerned that her anger would come through. She still had some work to do before she'd be ready to network and interview.

When something is new and frightening and the stakes are high, it's easy to assume the worst, and that becomes an obstacle. In Charlotte's case, she was convinced that the new employee had stabbed her in the back and set her up to lose her job. Along with this, she didn't want to have to look for a new job and was afraid that no one would hire her. This way of thinking was a trap with no way out, so she had to work through her anger, come up with a search map or plan, and make sure that her emotions were neutral while networking and interviewing. She had to be able to talk about her former company without smoke coming out of her ears.

The good news is that she did it. She worked hard, contacted other plumbing-supply companies, and in less than two months accepted an excellent offer.

Quick Do's and Don'ts

Do:

1. Realize that this might be a new experience for you and give yourself time to get used to it.

2. Ask for help. Whether you consult with a career counselor, a friend, or an in-transition group, get other opinions on both the process and how you specifically should position yourself in the job market.

3. Make sure to have a written schedule and a plan for your search. This isn't magic, but most people find that if they write down what they're going to do, it's a lot easier to do it without getting lost or discouraged. (See appendixes A and C for examples.)

4. Give your efforts enough time before you come to any conclusions. Answering three online ads, and then deciding after a week that it's pointless, is not a fair test.

Don't:

1. Spend a lot of time talking with former colleagues at your past company (whether they're still there or also let go) if the conversations are emotional and negative. You will only feel worse.

2. Listen to negative feedback that basically tells you you'll never work again. Unfortunately, this often comes from well-meaning friends and family members who are not experts on the job market.

3. Hang out with others who have given up.

4. Watch a lot of news. My rule is that you get a half-hour a day—that's it. Put yourself on a news diet. If you want to listen to radio programs or read the newspaper, that's usually just fine. It's the TV news that tends to dramatize unemployment issues.

5. Assume you know how your search will go. This is an unpredictable process, and even seasoned career counselors like me are often surprised. I tell my clients that I can't say when they'll be working again or where, but I can help them run a good, productive search that I know will get them to their goals more quickly.

Resources and Ideas

Some people find it helpful to draw on their own past experience, specifically how they got through other difficult times. Did they join a support group? Did they find books or audio resources that were helpful? Did they start walking five miles a day?

If your pride is hurt and you're having a difficult time getting past your frustration and anger, see if you can

- Look at the big picture. By this I mean seeing that what has happened to you isn't personal (although it feels that way). Realize that thousands of others have recently lost their jobs and have to go through the same process that you do.

- Find ways to take advantage of this involuntary change in your life. That could mean doing some career planning, helping an elderly parent, spending more time with your children, or simply giving yourself time to consider what you might want to do next.

- Consider that you might end up in a better job than the one you lost. I can't tell you how many times I've seen this happen, but of course it's hard to believe in the early days when you're stunned.

- Help someone else. By reaching out to another person who is in transition or by tutoring a child, you're getting your focus outside of your own situation. This often helps you gain perspective.

- Figure out how to build tolerance for the search process. It's easy to think you can just do it, but because there are often many ups and downs, it's good to consider who you know who's been through this recently, what groups might be helpful, and how you're going to create a schedule that you can sustain.

- Lastly, make your workspace attractive. I love flowers, so I try to always have a vase on my desk with roses or lilies or whatever is blooming in my garden. This makes it easier for me to get my work done.

CHAPTER 18

MYTH: I CAN'T ASK FOR HELP

I don't know if it's pride or some other form of misguided thinking, but one of the most persistent myths out there is that it's a terrible idea to ask for help. In fact, if you do it, you'll be seen as weak and miserable. People will laugh at you and talk about you behind your back. Your credibility will be shot.

Very few clients I've worked with will admit to this, but I often figure it out anyway: They won't ask for help.

So let's first look at what you shouldn't do when asking for help. Here are sample statements that will not motivate your network to help you:

- I need a job, please hire me.
- Here's my resume; could you please give it to someone at your company?
- I'm out of work and there are no jobs out there.
- You're still working, how come? My skills are better than yours.
- I can't believe I was let go. After all those years, how could they do that to me?
- I need a contact at XYZ company. Who do you know there?
- Thanks for the contact you gave me. I haven't heard from them. Can you follow up?

Alright, that's enough. Now for the flipside. Here are ways that you could ask for help that won't get you into trouble and should in fact motivate your network to action:

- I'm excited to be looking for a new position as a _____ (fill in the blank) and have put together a list of some companies I'm exploring. Could I share that with you?
- As I launch my search for a new position as a _____ (fill in the blank), I'm getting a few opinions to make sure I'm on the right track. Would you have time to sit down with me for 15 to 20 minutes so I could get your thoughts?

- I've had a few interviews recently, and part of the feedback I've received is that I may not be a fit for positions at this level. Could I get your help in sorting through this? I think I'm too close to see it clearly.
- I'm exploring an industry change as part of my job search strategy. Because you're in one of the industries I'm targeting, it would be really helpful to get your thoughts on how my background might be perceived by your industry. Would you have time for a short meeting to discuss this?

Okay, what's the difference? The messages in the first list are depressing and put a burden on the recipient. The statements in the second list clearly show a person in charge of his or her own career (and job search) who is asking for advice or input. They, in fact, compliment the recipient as being a person whose opinion matters. And perhaps most importantly, the questions in the second list are upbeat. They're optimistic. And strange as it may sound, what I've seen over and over again is that people like to help other people if they don't sound desperate or depressed, perhaps because they know they won't get stuck or burdened with more problems than they care to handle.

As I work with my clients on this, I demonstrate my "Girl Scout" voice. I try to sound professional and upbeat rather than manic. Confident. Some clients roll their eyes at me and groan. They say, "I can't sound like that; it's not me."

My answer: "That's okay. You don't have to sound like me, but you do have to sound motivated and positive. Let's hear it."

After more grumbling and telling me how tough I am, they do it—tentatively at first and then with more conviction. They hear their own voice sounding good—really good—and then they grudgingly admit that I'm right. They understand that this is the most effective way to approach others.

But what if you're having a really rotten day? What if everything is going wrong? (In my house it would be the cat throwing up on the rug, not being able to find important papers, no milk for my tea, and some critical appliance breaking down.) Then my advice is for you to do something else. This isn't the time for networking calls. For me, something physical almost always helps, whether it's a walk, doing the laundry, or washing windows.

If you're hesitant to ask others for help, flip it around and ask yourself how you feel when others approach you. Doesn't it make you feel good if you can assist someone in something they're doing? And, of course, a critical message in all this is that you're happy to reciprocate—now, later, whenever. This is another great motivator.

Lastly, remember that as you launch your search for a new job, you gain interesting information on things such as industry trends, who's hiring, what's typical in interviews, the best professional associations, helpful Web sites, and so on. And this information is gold—it's useful to those in transition as well as to those who are working. So as you ask for help, you gain knowledge that you can share, and your exchanges are a conversation, not a speech or lecture. Realizing this makes it a bit easier for many people to connect with others.

INSIDE THE BOX

Greg was in sales in the pharmaceutical industry. He had done pretty well, although he had experienced some turnover and had worked for five companies in the past nine years. During one break, he set up his own consulting practice. But it didn't do well, so he went back to working for a company with a large sales force.

We got the standard things done: resume, communications statements (why he's in transition, what he's looking for, key strengths, and so on), and networking and interview practice. Although I was aware that his employment history could have created a challenge, I was confident that he would land in a reasonable time frame because he had a solid background and was clearly successful in sales. He created his search map with a list of about 40 companies that fit his criteria. As we delved deeper into his networking methods, I discovered that he wouldn't ask anyone for help. He was convinced that this would make him look weak, and he was certain that the only way to get a job was to find it himself.

Then he did something that really surprised me. We were talking about targeting companies directly and how to break through the hiring bureaucracy so that he could come to the attention of the hiring manager.

"Oh," he said, "I set myself apart."

"How?" I asked.

"I'll show you next time."

A week or two later when we met again he brought a large bag into my office. I felt like a little kid at a birthday party—I couldn't wait to see what was in it. He pulled out a wooden box, basically a picture frame that was about three inches deep, and inside was his resume with a large gold star on it.

"I deliver this directly to the receptionist and tell him or her that if they want a gold star salesman, I'm the one."

I sat and looked at this and didn't know what to say. I was thinking it must take a lot of work to build this box and wondered what a hiring manager would say when given something so out of the ordinary. In other words, I was trying to fig-ure out if it would create a good way to stand out, or if he'd be seen as weird or desperate.

"Wow," I said. "That's really different."

"I've delivered about 10 of them so far," he told me.

"Any reaction?"

"The receptionists seem to like them."

"But what about when you follow up?" I ask.

"Can't get through with most, but with one hiring manager all he said was, 'Oh, you're the one with the resume in a box!' and then he said he had to run to a meeting but that he'd call me back. That was two weeks ago."

"Do you think that maybe it's overkill?"

He shook his head.

We then went back to our discussion about networking and why referrals are often the most effective way to get inside a company. He had a large network, and he had organized it in a spreadsheet. But he wouldn't e-mail or call them. It just wasn't done.

More weeks went by and he still didn't have an offer. His search went on longer than his previous ones had, and he grew discouraged. Again I urged him to find a way to reach out to his strong and diverse network, but for Greg, it wasn't done. By the time his program ended, he was still stuck inside the box.

Quick Do's and Don'ts

Do:

1. Find a way to get yourself to ask others for help. Understand that this isn't begging or burdening others; it's the way business is done.

2. Start with small steps. Find a contact who you know will be receptive and practice on them. With each person you talk with, you'll get better at this.

3. Discover your own style. The way you network and ask for help may be very different from the way I'd do it. That's just fine as long as it works.

4. Get support. Read books, listen to motivational speakers, and find out from others who have gone through this process how they did it.

Don't:

1. Give up before you begin. (I know I keep repeating this one, but it's something I see all the time.)

2. Assume you're bothering people.

3. Ask for too much too soon. The smaller the step, the more likely you are to get a "yes."

4. Expect too much. This is an unpredictable process and some people will be great and others won't. Don't let the duds bring you down.

Resources and Ideas

Because asking for help or advice is a central part of networking, which all career experts agree is the number-one job search technique (that is, the most effective and quickest way to a new job), if you're hesitant or having difficulty, it's critical that you find a way to do it.

- For some, reading books is helpful. My colleague, Orville Pierson, who wrote *Highly Effective Networking: Meet the Right People and Get a Great Job,* illustrates how important it is to be systematic in your networking and how it's part of your overall project plan for your search. He also addresses common misunderstandings and misconceptions about networking. Visit your local bookstore or library and read a few books on how others have learned this critical skill.

- This is a bit odd, but studies have shown that laughter not only heals but also helps us break through to new behaviors. One of my favorite films is *The Full Monty*. It's the story of out-of-work men in a mill town in England and the zany idea they hatch to regain their self-respect. I laughed so hard when I saw this film that my husband threatened to move to another part of the theatre. Rent it—it's great.

- Experiment. If you're still convinced that there is no way you're asking anyone for help, take a baby step and see what happens. But don't make a decision based on one attempt. This is a quirky process and you've got to talk to a number of people to get a good sense of how connecting with others works.

- Use e-mail or connecting through LinkedIn or any other social media sites as your first method. Many people find this much easier than making a call, and it's a great way to rebuild your network if you've let it slip. But please keep in mind that eventually it's going to be really important to also talk with people—on the phone and in person.

- Lastly, most of us will admit that we don't mind being asked for help ourselves. So if that's true, when you ask someone for advice or a job search–related favor, you're giving them a chance to feel good. Don't deprive others of this pleasure simply because you want to maintain control or are embarrassed to reach out. As I tell my team, "I've never had a client die from networking."

CHAPTER 19

LIE: I'LL HAVE A JOB BY MONDAY

A woman on the team I facilitate announced one week at our weekly meeting, "I'll have a job by Monday." She was desperate, at her wit's end, and I think she figured that if she made this public statement, it would happen—that she would be the next one to bring in donuts and ring the bell (as my clients do when they land a new job).

Someone asked her, "Are you going back for a second interview?"

"No."

"Well, where will you be working?"

Her answer: "It doesn't matter. But I'll be working by Monday."

The following week she showed up for the team meeting but didn't bring in donuts and didn't ring the bell. Her goal of finding any job, no matter where or what it paid, had failed. So now she had more discouragement on top of what had been there before. And her conclusion was *no one will ever hire me.*

Let me tell you a little bit about this person so that you understand her story better. She had worked for a major financial services firm in New York City and had been hired right out of college. Her first position wasn't that challenging, but her boss saw her potential: She's bright and creative and very good with people. So he promoted her. And for the nine years that she worked for that firm, this process continued until she progressed to a fairly high level of middle management.

But once she lost her job, she lost the structure that had supported her. Although she looked for similar positions at other financial services firms, she didn't really believe that she'd get hired at the level where she'd been when she was working. In other words, she quickly went from confident and believing in herself to the "I'll do anything" message that she had shared with the team.

After that last meeting (and no one asked her why she didn't have a job yet), she disappeared and never came back. She didn't return phone calls or e-mails. I found this incredibly sad. Here was a talented and smart person who was undermined by job loss. Everyone has setbacks—days when no matter what you do, nothing turns out right. But to throw in the towel because you can't tolerate the search process is letting job loss defeat you.

As I mentioned in chapter 11, you might decide, as I did, to take a lesser job just to be working again. But that's different from what happened here because in my case I knew it was a temporary strategy and it didn't have a timetable attached to it. So make sure, as you adjust your tactics in this process, not to create unrealistic deadlines. You've got plenty of pressure without giving yourself more.

SETTING A HIGH GOAL

Let's look at the story of another client who set a high goal for himself and how that worked out. This one is radically different from the woman on my team because there was no deadline involved and Rene learned how to sustain a long and challenging search.

Rene was part French and part Spanish, had lived in this country for many years, spoke fluent English, and was in finance at a senior level—just below CFO. For the first few months of his program, he had refused to come in; in fact, he used another service, which he paid for himself, to prepare his resume for him. Finally, when several interviews didn't lead to more interviews or an offer, he agreed to meet with me.

The first thing I noticed about him was how smart he was—smart and articulate. He drew diagrams to illustrate strategic plans that he'd been part of and clearly showed a passion for his work. As I probed, trying to get a sense of what had happened at his interviews, I got the impression that he felt the market (and more specifically the companies he had met with) owed him a job. He was insulted that they didn't get it and was further annoyed that the compensation, which is often one of the first topics of conversation, was not where he thought it should be. He told me that he was in his prime and didn't see why he should accept a lateral move or, even worse, a step down in what he earned. I listened, I waited, and then I asked him how long he'd been out of work. I knew the answer, but I was trying to make a point.

"Eight months," he said, and the confidence that he was projecting earlier was gone. He seemed tired and discouraged.

"That's a long time," I said.

He nodded.

I asked if he was open to contract work as a way to get back to work more quickly.

"No."

I was thinking that his compensation expectations might be stopping companies from exploring the next steps with him. Very carefully I suggested that he could soften his message and say something like, "I'm sure we can come to an agreement on compensation. What I'd like to focus on now, if it's alright with you, is how my international finance experience can help your organization."

And then, if pressed, he could have disclosed his past pay and explained that his current needs are flexible. Or he could have given a range that would work for both him and the company.

I saw him looking skeptically at me, so I did my best to explain that he couldn't let the frustration that is an inevitable part of the search process affect the way he interacted in networking and interviews. "Because we're selling ourselves, we've got to make a good impression. We've got to show interviewers that we're a good fit—that they'll be happy to have us as part of their organizations," I said. Lastly, I said that I thought openness and flexibility were positive characteristics, whereas a sense of entitlement was not. "We can have many different kinds of feelings, but we have to be careful with what we share. Interviewers are smart and usually can read these signals," I said.

The end of this story was amazing. Rene had 12 face-to-face interviews and finished in second place three times. He had 35 phone interviews. And most surprising of all, he turned down four offers because the fit, the pay, or, in one case, the location wasn't right. And with the offer that he accepted, he was able to almost match his previous salary. The scope of the new job was more challenging than his last one. He had held out for what was important to him because he was able to do this financially and had found a way to sustain a long search. Plus, he told me that he had learned from this process how important it was to have his life priorities in order, and that he now understood it was a job, not a lifelong commitment. Lastly, he was deeply motivated to help others. His final words to the new friends he had made during his job search were, "Contact me if you need any kind of help." And he meant it.

Quick Do's and Don'ts

Do:

1. Test your expectations with at least a few other people. These could include your compensation, your search timetable, your overall plan, or any other part of your campaign to find a new job.

2. Give yourself breaks and time off. Running a good job search is hard work, so make sure you're rewarding yourself and creating a schedule you can sustain.

3. Find the things that keep panic at bay. For some this may be exercise, for others volunteering or mentoring.

4. Adjust your plan to match your financial needs. Get good financial advice so that you can decrease your expenses while in transition. Some banks and community organizations offer free help.

Don't:

1. Let expectations narrow your market. No one wants to hire someone with an attitude.

2. Allow the ups and downs of looking for work make you bitter or demanding. Find ways to manage these feelings so that they don't get in your way.

3. Tell others that you'll have a job by Monday. That puts way too much pressure on you and also communicates to your network that you're desperate.

4. Set your goals so high that you can't reach them. You've got to have the financial resources and patience to sustain an extended job search if you aim high.

Resources and Ideas

Whether you're looking for a position just like your most recent one or are exploring new options, you want to set realistic goals and know how you're going to reach them. What resources might help you?

- One of my favorite resources is the public library. I'm not sure why it is, but once I walk in the door, I feel better. I like books, and I like people who like books. Maybe that's why. And during one of my own job searches, I volunteered at my local library putting books back on the shelves. I did this once a week for two hours for about two months and I loved every minute of it. My main challenge was not to start reading the books!

- Job search groups are often a good place to interact with others who are going through much of what you're experiencing. Look in your local paper, check churches and synagogues, and ask unemployment offices about groups that support job seekers. Just make sure that the group is well run (this means that it isn't a complaint session) and that it's attended by motivated people.

- Attend industry or professional organizations. I, for example, belong to the Association of Career Professionals and enjoy the meetings because I get to meet other career practitioners and the speakers are informative and help us stay up to date in our field. So if you're in the chemical industry, you can find organizations that support that industry, or if you're a marketer, there are groups that bring together people from this function. Use your reference librarian if you're stuck. Google is also helpful in finding what's out there. And as you read your local paper, pay attention to who has been promoted or just won an award. These might be good people to add to your network.

- Lastly, don't assume that others who are in transition can't help you. Many of my clients say to me, "Why go to that meeting—they're all out of work!" Of course it's good to attend meetings that include people who are working, but those who are looking for work may very well have contacts at some of the companies on your list. Don't assume that being out of work equals having no contacts. You're interested in talking to anyone, and help often comes from surprising sources. I've had clients get their jobs through their dry cleaners, hairstylists, and even their own children.

OBSTACLE: I'M OVERQUALIFIED AND EARN TOO MUCH

I've touched on the salary issue in a number of earlier chapters, but because this is a huge obstacle for many people in transition, I think it needs further exploration. How do you figure out what you're worth and what might knock you out of the running?

The first thing I look at is what a person knows about their market. If they've been with the same company for the past 28 years, they sure know the levels and salaries there. But now that they're thrust into a wider market, they need to figure out if they were overpaid, underpaid, or were pretty much in the middle. When I first started working as an outplacement counselor, we had a number of clients out of a telecommunications firm. What I learned about that company was that they often recruited candidates right out of high school, gave them excellent training, and promoted them. One of my clients was in accounts payable, and she was shocked to learn that other companies in the area (central New Jersey) weren't paying nearly as much as her previous company was. She had worked hard to get to her current level and had no intention of taking a step (or several steps) backward. But the market quickly taught her that she was probably going to have to compromise or else run a much longer search.

The second thing I consider is how up to date a client is in their function. If they're a programmer, for example, are they skilled and certified in the latest software applications? If they're graphic designers, are they current with the most recent enhancements to Dreamweaver, Quark, or InDesign? So as you figure out your own worth in the current job market, take a look at how up to date you are. If a company has to invest in training you, that might mean a lower salary—at least at the beginning.

Another factor that I consider is how effective clients are at selling themselves. In the past year I worked with a bright and motivated client in IT who was very difficult to understand. English was his second language, and although this didn't present a problem at his last job (as far as I know), it had become a huge hurdle in his search. We had practiced speaking slowly. I also helped him create an easy way to tell interviewers that he might be a bit hard to understand over the phone, but that in his work experience, communications were never an issue. And I had connected him with a language coach because I strongly believed that this was what was holding him back. (A company he recently had a face-to-face interview with told him that they wanted someone who was more of a leader. Again, I suspect that their doubts about him came from his heavy accent.) Even job seekers who were born in the U.S. and have no language issues may not be good at pitching themselves. (See chapter 36 for more on knowing your competitive advantage.)

When handling objections, I think it's really important to get down to the real issue. Sometimes when a company tells a candidate, "You're overqualified," what they mean is "you earn too much." Or, it could mean "you have better credentials than I do and there's no way I'm hiring someone who could take over my job!" It can also be a way of saying "there's no way you're going to stay here. This is probably a stepping stone for you and you'll leave as soon as you get another (and better) offer." And lastly, it can be an easy way to tell a candidate "no, thank you," without disclosing the real reason he or she wasn't hired. So if you can uncover what the true objection is, you at least will have a chance to address it. And sometimes you may choose to take what others perceive as a step backwards—whether that means earning less or accepting a position that isn't as senior as your last one—because you need to get back to work or are gaining other advantages such as experience in a new industry.

WHEN A STEP BACK IS A GOOD IDEA

One of my clients several years ago was a chemist who had been promoted several times until she reached the title of team lead. In this role, she was in charge of the other chemists in her department and monitored their work, made sure deadlines were met, and oversaw all the personnel issues that came up.

When she lost her job, she realized that she hated this role and had for some time. She liked chemistry and being a bench chemist, not being in management. She didn't care if she earned less—she wanted to be a scientist, not an administrator. As we worked on her strategy together, she came up with convincing examples from her past work that proved she was excited about being a chemist again. She wouldn't tell interviewers that she disliked being the team lead, but found positive ways to explain that for her, this wasn't a step backwards, but rather was a step in the right direction. She knew who she was and where she excelled. And what she had learned in her past role as team lead would make her even better at the bench.

She also knew that her compensation would be less, and after a careful budget review plus research on what bench scientists were making, she figured out what she needed to earn. This gave her a solid foundation when it came to negotiations and to interviewers' possible discomfort with her being overqualified for the position. She also understood that some interviewers would have a hard time believing that anyone would really be happy earning less than they did before.

Does this always work? Did everyone she interviewed with buy this story? Certainly not, but after about three months, she received an offer for a bench position and accepted it. For this chemist, a step backward (in both title and compensation) was a huge step forward. Her confidence in her own goals, and her concrete examples of why she preferred bench work, got her over the hump and back to work she loved.

Quick Do's and Don'ts

Do:

1. Talk to people in your industry who do work similar to yours, and ask about salary trends.

2. Use professional associations as a key way to stay up to date in your field—both in terms of skills and salary.

3. Develop relationships with recruiters, employment agencies, and contract firms so that you get a good sense of going rates for your type of work.

4. Research salaries using www.salary.com or www.Jobs-Salary.com and pay attention to the salary ranges you see in ads.

5. Develop strong accomplishment stories or examples that prove your worth and have a clear plan for what you want and need to earn. (Some clients aim high for the first several months of their search and then decide to compromise, while others, after careful research, stick with their initial goals.)

6. Defer the salary or compensation issue as long as you can so that you have a chance to prove your value before negotiating.

Don't:

1. Assume that your past salary is indicative of what other companies pay.

2. Be inflexible about your compensation. Salary is just one piece of the puzzle and you want to also pay attention to other perks. These might include work in a new industry or function, work that's close to home, flex hours or a virtual job, company day care, great benefits, a company car, and so on.

3. Sound as if the world owes you certain compensation. Although you might have worked very hard to get to where you are now, this isn't really of interest to the companies that want to hire you.

4. Use benefits as a negotiating tool. You may not need their benefits and think you might be able to trade them for something else. This rarely works because benefits are seen as a standard part of your package in most full-time jobs and often for those in which you work 20+ hours a week.

5. Become so fixated on what a small step backward might do to your overall career path that you refuse to see the plus side of an offer. One client on my team declared week after week that if anyone compromised on compensation,

they would never get back to their former worth. His search lasted well over a year.

Resources and Ideas

It's very hard not to define yourself by your compensation, and of course it's logical to see a raise as an indication of your value. This adds pressure to the already difficult task of evaluating and possibly negotiating a job offer. Here are some things to consider:

- A colleague and I once made a list of all the things you can negotiate. I think the list contained 47 items. I can't remember them all, but here are a few: number of vacation days, start date, when the benefits begin, when you'll have your first performance review, salary, sign-on bonuses, transportation allowance, a company car, other company equipment such as a laptop or BlackBerry, and so on. When considering an offer, try to look at the big picture, not just the salary. If it's helpful, make a plus and minus chart so that you have an easy way to see what you like about the position and what you don't.

- I tell my clients to make a list of the top three issues they want to negotiate and then narrow the list to two. They might be able to get all three, but I think it's helpful to know what you could give up if you need to. If a recruiter is involved, enlist their help. If not, wait until you have an offer firmly in hand—this means a written offer (e-mail is just fine) that has the critical information: title, start date, and salary. Then, with either HR or the person who will be your new boss, say that you're very excited about the position and are confident of the ways you can help the company, but that there are a few issues you'd like to discuss. Some people like to do this in person, while others are more comfortable over the phone.

- State clearly and simply that you'd like the compensation to be in the X to Y range, and if helpful, give one reason why. An example might be, "Given the scope of this position, managing operations both here and in Latin America, this is where the compensation needs to be." Don't overexplain or talk too much. This is like that old game of hot potato: Make your statement and stop talking. You've now passed the issue (the hot potato) to the other person and it's their problem, not yours. If you keep talking, you'll weaken your statement and will take back ownership.

- The biggest fear that I see in helping clients do this is their belief that they'll lose the offer. I've never seen that happen, but be careful. This means do your homework, know what other companies are paying for similar roles, narrow your requests to two to three things, remain positive and polite, and stop talking. In the end, you may not be able to negotiate. The first outplacement firm I worked for had set salaries and didn't change them no matter what rationale I offered. So it became, "do you want the job or not?" And I did, so I accepted a lower salary but then was able to get it back where I wanted a year later when I was downsized and then hired by another company. Without the experience that I had gained from this first company, that would probably not have happened.

- Find out from others how they've been successful in their negotiations, read a book or two about it (there are many, but I've listed a few in appendix H, "Suggested Reading"), and you'll be fine. Lastly, if you get two offers at more or less the same time, you have some additional leverage because you can use the offer from one company to see whether you can enhance the offer from the other. *Never* do this if it's not real—that is, never pretend to have an offer if you don't. It's way too risky. You could be told to take the other offer and then be left with nothing.

- If you're perceived as overqualified or as earning too much, try to uncover the real concerns and then address them. If they think you'll leave when you get a better offer, give them specific reasons why you're excited about this company and the role you'll play. Ask the hiring manager whether he or she has any concerns that you haven't addressed. And as you do this, make sure that your body language reinforces your message: You're a great fit and are excited about this opportunity.

CHAPTER 21

MYTH: THERE ARE NO JOBS IN THE SUMMER OR OVER THE HOLIDAYS

I love this myth because twice a year, my clients prove my other clients wrong. Those who think you can't get hired in the summer or in the November–December time frame are amazed when they learn of other clients in our office not only landing in these supposedly dead times in the job market, but also landing really good jobs. I'm probably a bit hard to take (that's a nice way of saying obnoxious) because I like to be right. And what I really like is to see the excitement and relief when someone who has worked hard and has struggled through this process knows that in a week or two, they'll be working again. It's awesome!

This belief that no one gets hired in the summer or over the holidays is hard to shake. I give my clients examples. I tell them that last year I had six team members land in December. I share with them how numerous clients tell me they got their last job in the summer or in December—and their eyes glaze over and I can see that they now wonder if I'm telling them the truth.

My guess is that the summer part of the myth comes from our educational system, when we have summers off and therefore still somehow believe, even after years of work, that nothing happens in the June-through-August time frame. It's harder to explain the holiday objection; again, those of us who have been working for a while know that things may be slow in the week between Christmas and New Year's, but business doesn't stop. But if it's true that this is at least a slower time, why not take advantage of it?

Try thinking of it this way: Let's say this myth is true and that hiring managers fall into a deep sleep and won't hire at these times. If you're out there working the job market when others aren't, you've still got an advantage. You have less competition. You'll stand out. And in addition, it's the people who are using summer barbeques and winter holiday parties to network who will be working sooner than those who give up and go to the beach or stay home and make cookies. So even if the job itself doesn't start until after the summer or the holidays, those who have given up will most likely not be the ones working when the season passes.

THE QUEEN OF NETWORKING

Here's an example from a former client whom I call the Queen of Networking. Liz had been downsized three times—in fact, three times in 10 years. She was in procurement at a senior level and was the ultimate people person. Networking to her was like oxygen: She had to have it. She was active at work and involved in her community, and she signed up to run things, such as the United Way campaign.

Liz looked at these supposedly dead times of the year as a great opportunity to connect with others. She sent out e-cards (using the blind copy feature so that no one knew that they were one of 70 people getting this card) to wish her friends a happy July 4th or Thanksgiving and to update them on her search. After wishing them a good holiday, she added a sentence or two saying something like, "My search for a Procurement Executive position is going well. I've been actively interviewing and am researching my top companies. I look forward to catching up with you."

While her message was open and a bit vague, she had basically let her network know that she hadn't landed yet and that she still needed their help. What happened after these blasts went out is that she got a flurry of e-mails back and then could go further in terms of enlisting her network's help. (Updating your profile on LinkedIn or filling in the short message box creates a similar campaign and is even easier.)

Liz was also genuinely interested in others, so her networking was always a give-and-take. She helped other clients who were starting their own businesses, she organized a fund-raising event for a friend whose child was seriously ill, and she started her own chapter of a nonprofit organization to support teenagers in her community. Talking to her was always interesting because she had a lot going on. And these other interests kept her connected and upbeat—and of course kept her network expanding.

Back to the myth. Liz understood that another reason networking might work particularly well at these times of the year is that people are in good moods—maybe because their workloads are a bit lighter or because they're enjoying the holiday season. She took advantage of this to connect with people, to keep them up to date, and to strengthen her network. In other words, she ignored this myth and proved, in each of her three searches, that jobs are found throughout the year.

Quick Do's and Don'ts

Do:

1. Tell yourself that you'll keep an open mind about when jobs are found and will at the very least experiment during your job search so that you can discover what works and what doesn't.

2. Follow Liz's example and take advantage of the summer or the holiday season to send out e-cards to your network.

3. Find ways to take advantage of special times of the year. This could mean inviting neighbors over for dessert and coffee, organizing an outing for your children and some of their friends, or helping a friend with a project. These activities should be fun, but are also opportunities to keep your network expanding and current.

4. Use evidence and not hearsay to determine your direction. Pay attention to what is working and what isn't in your search, and adjust your strategy. If all you're doing is answering ads and your phone isn't ringing, try something else. Go to a job seekers' meeting (you can find notices of these in your local paper or through the unemployment office), attend a professional association meeting, make a list of the top 10 companies you'd like to work for (*not* based on job postings), and see if you can find a contact in these organizations. Research the top three or four companies on this list and send a targeted e-mail to the hiring manager. (See appendix B for a template.)

Don't:

1. Let these myths lull you into sitting around. That is almost never a good idea in job search, except for short breaks that are a reward for strenuous activity.

2. Take others' opinions literally. People close to you, in an effort to be helpful, may say things like, "There are no jobs out there—especially now" or "Everyone is away for the summer." Again, you need only one job, and hiring happens all the time. The more you can pitch your skills to meet a need or solve a problem, the better your chances will be.

3. Stop. This is a process that takes preparation, persistence, patience, and courage. Keep at it. It's often very difficult to predict when and how you'll get your next job.

4. Expect instantaneous results. Most job seekers find that they have to lay the foundation before very much happens. So it might feel as if you're working really hard without any results, but very often this changes quickly. You can't give up. Work is too important both financially and personally.

Resources and Ideas

Behind many of the myths, lies, and obstacles that make looking for work harder than it needs to be is the pervasive belief that you shouldn't have to work to find a job. It should just be there so that when you lose your job, you step into another. This is especially true for those who found their last jobs in an easy market. So how can you get yourself to accept that you do have a job (and a critical one, at that), which is looking for a new job?

• Do something new. This could be a small step, such as rearranging your furniture, or something larger, such as taking up a sport or craft. These activities are energizing and will keep you from being trapped by the myths.

- Be open to suggestions. One sales client of mine said "yes" when a neighbor asked him to go for a bike ride on a hot summer day. They stopped off for water and to cool down with the neighbor's friend, and that led to a job offer.

- Interview someone whose skills and demeanor you admire and figure out what makes them successful. See what you can learn from him or her. (This also applies to written documents. I like to tell my clients that, unlike in academia, we encourage plagiarism—if you see a phrase in someone else's resume and it's true for you, borrow and adapt it.)

- Commit to the process. Recognizing that you have a job will help you through the inevitable ups and downs. Tell those close to you how they can help.

CHAPTER 22

MYTH: I'VE WORKED FOR ONLY ONE COMPANY, SO NO ONE ELSE WILL HIRE ME

I'm not sure if it would be accurate to say that the longer you're with a company, the worse it will be when you're let go. But I think it's fair to say that being with one company for a long time presents its own challenges. Most obviously, this has been your world. You may have grown up there if you started right out of high school or college. Often the company has invested in you and you were promoted, so there's mutual trust and respect. Your friends are people you met there. Your car gets you back and forth to work without any conscious effort on your part or your body has an internal clock timed to the exact length of your subway or bus ride.

What you're losing when you receive the dreaded message, "thanks for many years of loyal service but…," is a lot. And for people whose lives have revolved around this commitment (which is often those who worked hard and put a lot into making the company successful), it's particularly painful.

What you can't see is that although this was a job, a good job, and one you had for a long time, it's not the only job in the world. It's hard for most of us to view work as a cold contract: "You'll keep me as long as it makes financial sense; and when it doesn't, you'll let me go," or the flip side of that equation: "I'll stay as long as it makes sense, but it's my job to take care of or manage my career, so if something better comes along, I'll give two weeks' notice and be gone."

Here's a really difficult thing that I think is true for many of us: We stay in jobs we dislike because the known (even if it's not that great) is more comfortable than the unknown. Few people willingly hurl themselves into the dreaded world of job search, and a paycheck is a tough thing to give up.

Whether or not you enjoyed your most recent job, if you've been with your former company a long time, you have some extra work to do. There are many steps to take, but I like to have my clients start with the competition. I ask them to make a list of the companies in their geographic area (or in a wider area if they're open to relocation) that might be particularly interested in hiring someone from their previous employer.

Second, take a clear look at your skill set. Are you up to date, or do you need to invest in some additional training to be competitive in the market? One of the great benefits of enrolling in a course at your local community college or technical institute is that it proves you're motivated. When someone asks what you've been doing since you were let go, you have a strong answer. It's upbeat and positive. Although there's nothing wrong with an answer that is simply something like "I'm excited to be looking for a new position as a data-entry clerk or software engineer," you can hear the difference when the answer includes, "I've enrolled in a SQL course to make sure my skills are current."

As discussed in chapter 1, some of the early "how-to-get-through-the-shock-of-job-loss" suggestions may be helpful if you've been with a company for a long time. What I think is the most critical to remember is that you don't know the market and you don't know how to look for a new opportunity. You haven't had to look for work for a long time, and listening to the news or statistics from the Department of Labor probably won't motivate you.

See if you can take some small steps to get going in the right direction:

- Look carefully at your skills and take an inventory of what you're good at.
- Get familiar with some of the online job boards and such as Monster, Indeed, or CareerBuilder, so that you see what requirements are posted.
- Get to know a few employment agencies if you're interested in contract work (which can be a great way to get inside a company).
- Start researching recruiters if your goal is what I refer to as "the so-called permanent jobs."
- Make a list of companies that might be particularly interested in hiring people from your former one.

I've worked with many clients who have been with one company for 15 to 30 or more years, and with the steps mentioned in the preceding list, they've not only found new jobs, but they've also discovered that there can be advantages to working for another company. A recent client had her salary jump by $15,000, and others have found work that was more rewarding or closer to home. There is life beyond your past company.

HOW COULD THEY DO THIS TO ME?

Ben was stuck. He was so angry, he couldn't focus on anything except what his former company had done to him. Even before he was let go, he was in trouble. His performance reviews had slipped, he had been put on probation, and his boss had insisted that he get counseling for what was termed "an anger problem." He hated the counseling, hated his boss, and really hated his company, but he never thought that they would have the nerve to let him go, not after 22 years of service and some strong accomplishments. But they did.

He and I had first spoken on the phone. He had agreed to come to our orientation session but had sat through it stone-faced and unwilling to participate. I called to follow up a few days later, and he had a lot to say—all about what his company had done to him. I listened, and after a while asked him what he thought would help get the focus on what he needed to do now. I mentioned that looking for work is a job and that I'd like to help him put together a strong resume, review networking and interview preparation skills, as well as show him how to balance his search between what we call the published and unpublished job markets. He wouldn't agree to meet with me.

I tried a week later to see if he would come to the team meeting that we hold weekly. I thought it might be motivating for him to witness what others were doing in the search process. He agreed to come but didn't show up. When I called him again, he said he'd come the following week. But then he called me on the morning of the team meeting to tell me that he couldn't come because he was having computer problems.

This is where the job search process defeats you. If someone can't get past the pain and anger and disappointment, it may not be possible to find another job, or certainly to keep it. The anger is too toxic and it scares potential employers. It has to be worked through. When I mentioned counseling as a possible resource to Ben, he let me know that he'd been forced to go through counseling once and would never do it again. After that he wouldn't return my calls, so I don't know what happened. I really hope he found a way through this.

Quick Do's and Don'ts

Do:

1. Take advantage of all the resources you can that will help you process your job loss and get you ready to manage a successful search.

2. Think about how you've made it through other difficult times in your life and rely on the strategies that helped. (Yoga got me through some tough times at one phase in my life. And after my mother died, weight training gave me a focus and new friends—plus some really good arm muscles.)

3. Keep your mind open to ideas that might seem surprising. I always tell my clients that they're in the driver's seat, but by meeting with a seasoned career coach who shares what has worked for others, their search can be more productive.

Don't:

1. Decide you know the outcome of your search before you begin. You don't; I don't; no one does.

2. Let anger or disappointment dominate your communications. You could say, "I was really upset to lose my job at XYZ company after 24 years, but I've come to realize that I gained excellent skills that I'm excited to offer to another company in the [fill in the blank] industry." What's good about this message is it's positive while still honest. And even if you're not excited, say it anyway; eventually, you will be. This is one of the rare times when I think it's just fine to lie.

3. Assume you know the job market. If you've been with one company for a long time, you know that company, not the wider market. Do your homework before you come to any conclusions.

Resources and Ideas

Job loss presents a challenge for most people who experience it. After many years with one company, the loss may be even harder to process. Here are a few suggestions that have helped my clients:

- Numerous studies have demonstrated the healing power of laughter. Although I'd never say this at an interview (or at least not until I felt pretty comfortable), my colleagues at work tell me that the one thing they notice is that I laugh a lot. My feeling is that it's really necessary in a difficult process to find things that can lighten the load. When, for example, one of my clients born in India received notice that he had to file with the Selective Service, we spent weeks laughing about his new career in the military. (He wasn't a citizen, so of course he wasn't supposed to register for the U.S. military.)

- Another difficult to define but important resource is comfort. One of the best memories I have of the day my mother died is our dog—a wonderful collie-shepherd mix—climbing into bed with me. He plunked his 80 pounds of fur and love and silence right next to me and let me wrap my arms around him. That was exactly what I needed. So in addition to finding things that make you smile, be aware of what comforts you. It could be a hot bath, a long chat with a friend, playing basketball, helping a neighbor, or reading a good book.

- Make sure to schedule things on your calendar every week that you can look forward to. It could be as simple as taking your dog to a new park, trying out a recipe, going to a baseball game, listening to music you really like, or making a loaf of bread for a neighbor. These simple things are an important part of the healing and balance that can help you stay motivated and positive in your job search.

- Keep expanding your world. Many people get so focused on finding their next job that they ignore everything else around them. Get out of the house, do different things, play with your children (or with the neighborhood kids if you don't have children), and cultivate your curiosity. It's a winning trait that will also motivate others to help you.

- If you're worried about getting hired by another company, remember that you must have been successful to have been retained by your former company for so many years. You have a solid track record that you now can offer to others.

CHAPTER 23

LIE: I DON'T HAVE TIME
TO LOOK FOR WORK

As you can probably guess, many people become disorganized when they lose their jobs. The structure and pressure of working forced them to figure out how to get a lot of other things done, including caring for children or pets or aging parents, grocery shopping, keeping up with the laundry, and so on. So the double whammy is you're thrown into an unfamiliar process and your structure is gone. As one client said to me, "It's so overwhelming. Why get out of bed?"

And my simple answer is, "You have to. You can't let job loss defeat you." And it's not just about money or your financial needs. Even those who receive a year's severance need to decide what they want to do and then find a systematic way to get there. Otherwise, you've let a company determine your fate, and that's handing over power that should be yours.

But can you enjoy some things that you weren't able to do when you were working? Absolutely. For example, let's say you have a two-year-old who goes to daycare every day. Maybe you pick up your child early a few afternoons a week and go to the playground. (Think carefully before you cancel your childcare altogether. It takes time to run a good search.) Or, as mentioned earlier, you might learn a new skill or take up a hobby that you never had time for. A client I recently worked with cooks once a month for the Ronald McDonald House. She not only gets to prepare a good meal for families with seriously ill children, but she also gets to know and support them. Because the same group has been preparing these meals together for a while, she has made close friends with the other volunteers.

What I'm saying here is that you can allow yourself some flexibility, but if several weeks go by and your resume is still in draft form, you need to create a schedule and stick to it. Here's an example:

8:00–9:30: Check e-mail, major job boards, and top company Web sites.

9:30–11:00: Review your networking spreadsheet to see who needs a follow-up call or e-mail and reach out to five new contacts.

11:00–11:30: Break time. Walk the dog, run on the treadmill, or have a snack (or do all three at once!).

11:30–12:30: Research top companies and write a draft of a tailored target e-mail (see appendix B for a template).

12:30–1:30: Break for lunch or errands.

1:30–3:00: Research professional associations, industry groups, or job search support meetings and sign up to attend their meetings. (Note: If you need to end your day here, include some of the networking mentioned in the 3–5 p.m. time slot. You've put in five and a half hours of work, which is enough to produce good results if you do it at least five days a week.)

3:00–5:00: Review your networking contacts (including LinkedIn) to see whether you can find a contact at your top companies. Think about what you've accomplished this day and prioritize what you must do tomorrow. Write this down so it's the first thing you'll see when you report to your desk tomorrow.

If the preceding schedule is too rigid for you, take a look at a few others in appendix A, where you'll see a weekly version as well as a monthly one. From my experience, looking for work is a slippery process, so any steps you can take to provide structure and accountability will pay off. Follow a schedule similar to this, search "smart," (meaning that you don't get stuck answering Internet ads all day), and you'll be productive and will move forward. The preceding schedule gives you seven-and-a-half hours of work a day that you should do at least five days a week. That gives you a 37.5-hour work week—which is still less than what many people have when employed. (Some job seekers get this down to five hours a day, which gives them a 25-hour work week. Be careful if you invest any less time than this; your search may take longer.)

If your family or friends keep calling you during your job search work times, share your schedule with them and explain that this is your job right now. If friends still don't get it, screen your calls and then call them back during a break or in the evening. Of course, if there's an emergency, you have to take care of it. But when things settle down, see if you can make up some of the time, perhaps in the evening after the kids are asleep. There is something seriously wrong if you really need a new job but are spending only a few hours a week searching.

Lastly, educate those close to you so that they understand that looking for a job *is* a job—and a critical one, at that. Don't assume that your family will get it without effort on your part. I've found, in my work with thousands of people in transition, that the spouse of the person who has been downsized is often more anxious than the job seeker. Share what you're doing, set up a schedule, let them know ways they can help, and explain why you need uninterrupted time.

JUST DANCE

Betty was in her early 30s and was in marketing. To say she was highly motivated was an understatement. She was the ultimate list maker, worked hard, and called herself a workaholic. So when she and I had met a few times and her resume and job search map were completed, I thought to myself, "She is going to sail through this." In addition, she was a really nice person and connected well with others, so I knew she would make a good impression when she interviewed.

But at about the two-month mark, she was stuck. She was brought up short because she didn't see any results. She asked me, "Why isn't my phone ringing? Is anyone out there?" And I did my best to explain that she had worked hard to create a foundation that was going to get results, but that it was difficult to say when.

She didn't have a daily schedule (such as the one earlier in this chapter) and was certain she didn't need one. She was putting in at least eight hours a day and often worked on her search over the weekend. So I asked her a question that surprised her: "What are you doing for fun?"

"What?" she asked.

"I understand you're working really hard, but this is a tough schedule to maintain. Could you go to a movie some afternoon or have lunch with a friend?"

She frowned at me and I could see that she was wondering why on earth I would suggest such a frivolous thing. As we talked further about this, I found out that she loved to dance. Putting on some old rock 'n' roll when no one else was home, cranking up the volume, and dancing made her feel really good.

"Could you do that for 10 minutes once a day?"

"But I need a job."

"Yes," I said, "I know that, but you also need to take care of yourself. So in addition to balancing your search methods (we had talked at length about networking, targeting, not getting stuck on the Internet, and so on), you've got to find ways to keep yourself upbeat and motivated. Dancing 10 minutes a day isn't going to cost you anything, so could you just do it, or at least go out for a walk?"

She looked at me and didn't answer.

"Could you try it for a week?"

She nodded.

And because she was open to new ideas, even ones that seemed strange to her, she did it. She added walks and dancing to her search schedule. And she felt better. And then the phone started to ring (not because of the walking or dancing). She was refreshed and present and did a good job talking about her background. That led to a wonderful offer. In the end, I'm sure it was her dedication and hard work that got her there, but maybe the dancing helped, too. Hard to say.

Quick Do's and Don'ts

Do:

1. Figure out what it takes to be able to put in a good 25 to 30 productive hours a week on your job search. (There are exceptions to this time commitment, but make sure that if you're spending less time per week on your search, you're focusing on the most productive methods.)

2. Make a daily, weekly, or monthly schedule and refer to it. Adjust it as necessary.

3. Educate your support system so that they understand your plan and your schedule. Do your best to minimize distractions. (I, for example, have trained my family and friends never to call me in the morning because that's my best writing time.)

Don't:

1. Fall into bad habits. They're often hard to break. Even if you don't feel like it, see if you can get yourself into a productive schedule from the start.

2. Give up before you start. I can't tell you how many clients have told me that there are no jobs out there when they haven't started looking for one.

3. Let nonessential activities eclipse your job search. The dishes will get done, the bedroom will get painted, the gutters will be cleaned, but not during your search time.

Resources and Ideas

What else might help you if you're struggling with the time issue and wonder how you ever had time to work?

- There are tons of time-management resources, including videos, CDs, classes, books, and so on. See whether you can find some that help you manage this demanding and time-consuming process.

- Talk to others who are also looking for a new opportunity and ask them how they're managing their time. Do they have a schedule? Will they share that with you?

- Create your schedule and figure out how you're spending your time. Keep a careful log so that if you say, "I worked really hard on my search today," but you spent only two hours on it, you'll see the disconnect.

- Evaluate what's a good use of your time and what isn't. Should you, for example, drive an hour and a half in the pouring rain to go to a job fair? Probably not, because job fairs tend to focus on entry-level jobs and many times don't yield much except this really frustrating advice: "Apply to positions on our

Web site if you're interested." However, if you haven't been in the job market for a long time and need to get a sense of the conditions, it could be a good idea.

- Be protective of your time, pay attention to what lifts your spirits and what doesn't, and evaluate your search methods so that you can do more of what is productive and less of what isn't.

- Remember that looking for work is like running a business, and you have to play all the roles: CEO, CFO, COO, marketing, administration, and so on. By managing these diverse functions effectively, you'll become visible in the marketplace and reach your goal.

CHAPTER 24

MYTH: I CAN'T GET A JOB
IF I DON'T HAVE A JOB

This myth is like a burr: Once it's stuck on your socks, you can't get it off. It has a life of its own and shows up in my office on a weekly basis. I do my best not to scream when, in going over a resume, the client tells me in no uncertain terms that they're unemployable because they're unemployed.

So, trying not to sound hysterical, I ask, "How do you know?"

This is usually met with a blank stare.

Again I ask, "How do you know companies won't want to hire you because you're in transition?" (I hope you noticed that I snuck in the "in transition" phrase instead of "unemployed.")

"Well," they say, "that's the way it works."

"But when's the last time you looked for a job?" I ask.

"Twenty years ago."

"So what you're telling me" (I can feel my blood pressure skyrocketing as I say this), "is that no one who is out of work could ever get hired because only people who are working get hired. Is that right?"

Now there is a moment of hesitation as they think I've led them into a trap. I haven't, but I'm doing my best to debunk this myth. I take a deep breath and talk about the thousands of clients I've worked with—in good economies and bad—and how a very high percentage of them have landed new jobs. No one gives up this myth easily, but many times, after a month or so of working with us and learning about the job search process, it loses its hold on them. They see others landing good jobs. They hear people in our classes or team meetings speaking confidently about their prospects. And as the phone begins to ring and they experience interest from companies or recruiters and expand their network, they start to believe that they could indeed get hired despite their current status.

A lot of these same people also subscribe to this related myth: "The longer my search takes, the more trouble I'm in." Well, that depends on a lot of things. Let's say you live in New Jersey and have worked in manufacturing. But now manufacturing is being done either overseas or in other, less expensive parts of the country. Then you could expect your search to take a while because there are fewer manufacturing jobs available and you might have to invest in training to try another industry or function. Or if your skills aren't up to date, your search could take longer because there's tremendous pressure to stay competitive. So a shrinking market or having outdated skills could hurt you much more than being in transition for a few months.

If, for example, you're a programmer who has worked only in mainframe environments, you're facing a shrinking market and you might be perceived of as a kind of dinosaur. So while you're looking for companies who still use mainframes, you might also need to invest in training that will expand your competencies and job possibilities. Remember that being in transition doesn't knock you out of the market, especially if you can explain what you're doing and why it may be taking a while. (And, of course, the way you communicate this is essential so that you come across as motivated and confident.)

If you think of job searching as a fishing expedition, you want to make sure there are lots of fish in the pond—not just one or two. Anytime you can increase your chances, whether by being willing to move or expanding where you'll work, or through acquiring additional skills or transitioning to a new industry, it's a good idea. So, back to the timing issue: Will it hurt you if you're out of work or in transition for three months or six months or a year? Will you become less employable? Yes and no.

Where I think it's safe to say being out of work becomes a negative is when it drags you down. As we've discussed earlier, job loss is a loss of structure, paycheck, and many times your friends or social context. It's hard not to feel powerless and lost. And when this happens, your message to your network and in interviews becomes negative. This creates a huge challenge because very few employers want to hire someone who comes across as angry, discouraged, or bitter.

If, on the other hand, a job seeker's message is this:

> *Manufacturing has been hard hit in our area, so I've decided to improve my skills as a production line supervisor and I'm currently enrolled in classes to help me break into the XYZ industry where my manufacturing background could be a plus.*

the message conveys determination, intelligence, and a willingness to be flexible. Even enrolling in classes that don't directly apply to a specific function or industry is a good sign because it makes you look motivated and smart.

I'LL NEVER WORK AGAIN

I have two nicknames at work. One is "the warden" and the other is "grammar police." Both are probably self-explanatory, but I want to tell you how I got the warden title. It involves a client who was 100 percent convinced that he would never work again. And that belief was an obstacle that he wasn't able to get around.

Alan was in facilities. He had a high school education, received good training on the job, and was let go after 15 years. After we got through some of the basics and had his resume completed, we came to a standstill—or more accurately, an impasse. He liked his new resume, was open to posting it on the major job boards, and was busy answering ads. But that was where he drew the line because he believed that he wouldn't get hired unless he already had a job. So one day, as I was trying to get him around this myth, he had a smirk on his face.

"What's funny?" I asked.

"Nothing."

"Oh, come on. I can see that something is cracking you up."

He hesitated and then told me that he thought of me as his parole officer.

"What?"

"Not that I've been in jail," he added quickly. "But coming in here, meeting with you, going over what I've done, I feel like I'm reporting to some kind of authority—like I'm on parole."

I hesitated for a second and then burst out laughing. Alan laughed, too, maybe relieved that I wasn't angry. Later that day, as I mentioned this story to my team (not mentioning his name), a client who had started her own career working in a correctional facility told me that I wasn't a parole officer, I was the warden. She even made a plaque for me that to this day hangs in my office. In addition to my name and my new title, "The Warden," there's clipart of a person in leg irons and a slogan: "Take those shackles off your job search." I'm very proud of this.

Back to Alan. I looked forward to my meetings with him because I could see he was bright and of course had a nice sense of humor. Despite those characteristics, I couldn't get him to believe that his search could result in an offer, and so he limited his activity to answering ads. I threw statistics at him, showed him ways to pitch himself directly to hiring managers, talked about the power of networking and how simple it was, and told him success stories about other clients who had been both proactive and creative. We discussed contract work as a way to break into a company or a new industry and why it could be easier to get than permanent positions. In our final meeting of his three-month program, I could see that he still believed he would never work again because he wouldn't be able to find a job if he didn't have one. The best I could do at that point was to leave the door open.

"Call me," I said, "if you change your mind. Or if you have a question. Okay?"

He nodded, we shook hands, and I never heard from him again.

Quick Do's and Don'ts

Do:

1. Find a way to accept that being out of work is not a liability. Especially in the current economy, almost no one will ask why you're in transition.

2. Practice a simple explanation of what happened at your most recent company. Many times these explanations include plant closings, consolidation, mergers and acquisitions, loss of sales, a drug going generic, and so on.

3. Focus on what you have to offer, not on what you've lost.

4. Conduct your own survey and talk to people who have been out of work but who are now working again. How did they get hired?

Don't:

1. Let your emotions cloud your vision. Job loss often packs a wallop, but your task now is to not let it harm you. This is an excellent time to think about your career, evaluate the kinds of work you enjoy, and plan your search around both doable and interesting goals.

2. Fall into the trap of believing you need a job to get one. Why have you suddenly become less employable? Have your skills deteriorated? If they have, do something about it. (This is particularly important in areas that are changing rapidly, such as technology.)

3. Convey a negative message. One of the great ironies of this process is that if you sound like you really need help, you'll scare people off. Most of us like to help people when we feel we'll get good results.

Resources and Ideas

Because this myth is so pervasive and powerful, here are a few additional ideas to help you get beyond it.

- It isn't easy to change. My job as a career coach for an outplacement firm has taught me that most of us are at least a little afraid of the unknown. We cling to things that really aren't working (a terrible job, a bad relationship, and so on) because the known, even if it's not that great, feels better than facing the unknown. Paycheck trumps no paycheck. And we work really hard to convince ourselves that the situation isn't really that bad, or that next week or next month it will change for the better. Recognizing that you've been thrown into a situation with a lot of change could help you address it head on and not cling to the past or myths that make it very difficult to believe you'll work again.

- Courage helps. So whatever can you do to build yourself up is a good investment. It will get you through the rough times when you've interviewed for a job you'd love and then hear nothing for three weeks. It will sustain you through the ups and downs and reversals that are an inherent part of this process. It will help you know that you have a lot to offer and that in time, you'll meet the right person at the right company who will get it.

- If you knew that you'd have a wonderful job in three months or whenever, you would be able to tolerate this unpredictable process better. At work we usually get to see the results of our efforts, whether large or small. Things are logical: You do this and such and such happens. Looking for work, however, isn't like that. You make a good effort and nothing happens. You have an inside contact and the person at the company won't call you back. It's a bit like Alice in Wonderland—you feel lost and wonder who wrote the rules. There's a great deal you can't control, but the flipside of this is that there's a lot you can.

- Focusing on what you can control needs to be your anchor: Here's what you're doing and why, and if that doesn't work, you'll go to plan B. You have a plan and you work it. You search smart. You're open to new ideas and learn from others, whether or not they're looking for work. And you have a way to measure progress. This is not an all-or-nothing game. Small steps are usually what get you to an offer—a lot of small steps, including detours and dead ends, things that fizzle out, and wonderful surprises that come out of nowhere.

- Don't add to these challenges by believing that you are now unemployable if you're in transition. I've never seen any data that supports that assumption, and when a company asks you when you can start your new job, you don't have to give two weeks' notice. You're available now!

CHAPTER 25

MYTH: I CAN'T GET HIRED AT XYZ COMPANY BECAUSE THEY JUST DOWNSIZED

If you had my job, if you worked with hundreds of people of all functions and levels from the moment they are laid off to the start of their new jobs, it wouldn't be difficult for you to see that companies are like revolving doors: out on one side, in on the other. So although consolidations or mergers and acquisitions may mean that companies are laying off employees, in my experience they often hire at the same time. You might want to say, "That's crazy!" and I'd agree with you. But crazy or not, it happens all the time.

Related to this myth is the posting phenomenon—meaning that a huge majority of job seekers judge the market by what's posted. So let's say a person has worked successfully in the pharmaceutical industry and perhaps lives in an area such as New Jersey (or Boston or California) where large pharma and growing biotech companies are located. And let's say that he really wants to work for a particular leading pharmaceutical firm. He goes to the company Web site, checks out job postings, and then tells me that not only are there no postings in his area, but it's also obvious the company will never hire anyone again because just last week they eliminated 4,000 employees.

So now he's trapped by two pieces of misinformation: that the postings are an accurate indication of hiring and that layoffs are a sure sign that he himself can't get hired there. In my head I'm thinking, "Wrong, wrong, wrong!" But understanding that this is all new to my client, I ask questions to try to help him get around these obstacles.

"Did you experience other layoffs at your company before you were let go?" I ask. Most say that they did.

"And do you know if people were also hired or brought into the company at the same time?" I usually get a little nod.

"So one thing doesn't really seem to affect the other, does it?" Here I get a shrug.

"Okay, so let's just say we don't know whether some companies, when they're reducing their workforce, will bring in new people. Would that be fair to say?" (This is when I start wondering if I should have been a lawyer. There are really few things more satisfying than a good argument.) I get a dull stare or a "Whatever."

"So try to think of layoffs as change, and change can be good. Change means that doors may open, that new jobs may be created, that perhaps people are being promoted—and that could mean an opportunity will open that will be just right for you."

"Okay, but how do I know about them?" the client asks.

"Great question. The short answer is by talking to people inside the company—what is often referred to as networking. Your goal is to get in front of hiring managers whether or not they have a need, so that if they do or when they do, they'll know about you. Even if they don't have an opening now, they might in a week or a month. Before you end your meeting (and this really is a meeting, not an interview), you'll ask whether it's okay to stay in touch. So once every few weeks, you send this person who would be your boss a quick e-mail, an article about the company, or anything relevant so that you don't fade into oblivion."

Now I realize that I've been talking too much. And even worse, I'm sounding bossy, so I quiet myself down and see what the client has to say. Many times I'm asked, "But why would a busy hiring manager see me? What's in it for them?" Look at the example in the following sidebar for an answer.

GETTING TO HIRING MANAGERS

This example is from my own career. In 1994 I landed my first job in the outplacement industry because my neighbor, who got tired of hearing me whine about how I didn't want to be a corporate trainer anymore (even though I was very good at it), thought I'd be good in his field: outplacement. He was nice enough to introduce me to the key players at his firm. I met several people and visited two of their offices, but because my resume screamed "corporate trainer," they decided that the best way to use me was in a training role. I needed to work and liked the company, but I knew in my heart that I wasn't going to last in a training role. I had trained more than 10,000 middle and senior managers in the preceding six years with my former company and needed to do something else, especially because the travel had worn me down.

To this day I don't know how this happened, but a woman from the outplacement firm called me and asked me what kind of role I was interested in. I told her that I really wanted to do the one-on-one counseling work. I was very happy to have training as part of my job, but I wasn't interested in 100 percent training. She laughed and said that the men always got things wrong and that she'd take care of it. She did. So before I knew what was happening, I had my first job with a wonderful firm 18 miles from my home. I went through the initial training, and every day was an adventure as I learned new ways to help my clients through the transition process. And at our weekly staff meetings, I received support and guidance from the more seasoned staff.

Fast-forward one year and it was my birthday. I was given a cake. An hour later my boss called me into his office. I was on a sugar high and was feeling really good.

"I'm sorry, Jean," he said, "but we've got to cut our staff and because you were the last in, you'll be the first out."

"What?"

He repeated his message, but it didn't make any sense. And then all I could think to say was, "On my birthday?"

"Well, that was unfortunate, but this is a business decision…."

I stopped listening. It didn't matter what I said or what I did or even what I'd put into my work. I was being let go. Somehow I got out of his office, made it through the rest of the day, and finished out the two weeks to my end date. It was awful. I cried on my way home in the car. I shouted terrible things in imaginary conversations with this boss who I had previously admired. Not anymore.

But in a way, I was lucky. My year with that firm gave me two things: a foothold in an industry that I love and tools for running a really good search. As I considered how I was going to get my next job (and I wanted to stay in the same role in the outplacement industry), I realized that there would be no postings because I'd never seen an ad for a job in my field. I also knew that recruiters weren't likely to work in my industry because it was too small. And networking was a bit tricky because outplacement firms are highly competitive with each other, so I wasn't sure that I could get help from people who might perceive me as coming from the enemy camp. That left targeting, which is basically going directly to a hiring manager at a company of interest. This technique put me in a good place because I knew I could write a strong letter that would hopefully get me in the door for a discussion. (This was 1995—still in the era of snail mail.)

I found 15 firms within my geographical range, did careful research on my top six, and staggered the letters so that I could follow up promptly. Within two weeks, I had five interviews. Those led to two offers; I accepted the best one and started my new job. Two years later, we were bought out by Lee Hecht Harrison, my current employer. And that's where I've been ever since.

I paid attention to what I learned about the firms I was targeting, but didn't let staffing changes or talk of a hiring freeze deter me from trying. And I found a successful way to get to the person in each firm who could see what I could contribute and make the decision to hire me. And lastly, because I also understood that on some level this is a numbers game, I targeted enough companies to generate good results.

Quick Do's and Don'ts

Do:

1. Make your market as wide and open as possible. Don't dismiss a company because they're laying people off or haven't posted positions.

2. Be inclusive rather than exclusive. You have no idea how many clients have said to me, "I only want to work five minutes from my home." This sets you up for failure before you've even begun to search.

3. Tap into your creativity and get others to help you brainstorm, whether in making your list of companies to pursue or your overall job search strategy.

Don't:

1. Watch or read a lot of news. Statistics about a depressed job market will not motivate you. But being informed is really important, so pay attention to your research to make sure that your job market is expanding.

2. Assume that you know what will work or what won't work until you've put some effort into the process. If you have access to a career counselor, take advantage of that resource. We know a lot about the job market and can help you.

3. Let layoffs or downsizings stop you from investigating a company. Recently I've had quite a few clients rehired by the companies that just let them go. Keep your list open and don't rule out opportunities until you've made a really good effort.

Resources and Ideas

Why would a busy hiring manager see you? Let's look at this question more carefully here in the context of pervasive and frequent downsizings.

- A busy manager with a demanding schedule doesn't have the luxury of wasting time. But you can help this person by understanding what their business problems are and providing a solution. By researching companies carefully and then offering help, you might get in the door.

- Referrals are golden. They're the keys that open doors that are difficult to open. A busy manager will see you because you're been referred in by one of his or her employees, a friend, or someone else whose opinion matters.

- You're saving them time and money. If the department needs a new programmer, and you show up with the skill set that they need, you've saved them a huge hassle: advertising the position, sorting through resumes, weeding out the top candidates, interviewing, and so on. And there's no fee involved when you walk in the door on your own.

- Curiosity is another factor. Many hiring managers want and need to know "what's out there?" You bring experience from the company or companies you've worked for, as well as knowledge of the job market. These can be a huge help to them.

- If your past experience hits the bull's-eye that your target company is looking for (you initiated a program, performed training, or launched a program in Asia), you can hit the ground running and won't require the usual startup time that most employees need. Smart hiring managers keep their doors open for this reason.

CHAPTER 26

MYTH: I CAN'T GET A JOB IN THAT INDUSTRY BECAUSE I DON'T HAVE EXPERIENCE IN IT

Myths that contain a kernel of truth are the most difficult to fight. And this one is a prime example. Some industries are what I call myopic. They refuse to consider anyone who doesn't have a strong track record in their particular industry, even though we all know that finance is finance, operations is operations, human resources is human resources, and so on, no matter what the industry.

So with this particular challenge, I tell my clients to look for the "first cousins" or closely related industries that might be a bit more open. So let's say you want to work in the pharmaceutical industry but have no work history in it. You might find opportunities in healthcare, with a biotech firm, or even in medical devices because they're a bit more open. And once you have that experience, you might be able to break into pharma.

This brings us back to the hiring process. Almost everyone has seen this happen more than once: A less-qualified candidate gets the job. Why is that? What would make a company turn down someone who is perfect and hire someone else who might need a lot of training or who has never worked in the industry? One answer to these questions is "the intangibles," or what is often called "fit." What are these and how can you make them work for you?

I designed and teach a class called The Interview Video Lab. In it we cover the physical aspects of interviewing, including posture, gestures, voice, eye contact, handshake, note taking, facial expression, and so on. And I always start the class by asking, "How long do you have to make a first impression?" I don't know the exact answer to this question, but I do know that it's not long. I tell the class that when I lived in New York City and was walking back to my apartment at night, my sensors were on high alert. I was aware of who was around me, which stores were open, and whether it might be a really good idea to cross the street. I wasn't afraid, just aware. (Okay, there were times when my heart beat like crazy, but I never had a problem and always made it home just fine.) So whether these rapid assessments are accurate or not, we're wired to make them of other people as part of our survival instincts.

From the moment you walk into a building for an interview or a networking meeting, you're "on." You're ready to present your best self. You smile and give a firm handshake when the person comes to meet you. (We all know how distracting that limp-fish kind of handshake is.) You look happy to be there, even if you're terrified. And then you do your best to get the focus on them—what they need, how your background could help, what their greatest challenge is, and so on. You tell the truth. And if you don't have a skill but know you could learn it easily, you give an example of how you did that in the past.

So in addition to your specific background, you're selling enthusiasm, intelligence, interest in them, motivation, and curiosity. These are the intangibles that can move you to the top of the pile and even get you hired over a person with a stronger resume. Why? Because we want to work with people we like. We're swayed by the intangibles. And many hiring managers like to discover potential. You'll make them look good.

This doesn't always happen, by any means, and one client on the team I run keeps frustrating herself by applying for jobs where she matches only about 40 percent of the requirements. I don't think that's a good idea. There's plenty of discouragement in this process already without setting yourself up for more.

So back to industry experience. Include the first cousins of the industries you're targeting. As you talk to people in those industries, ask what skills you would need to be seen as a good fit. Read industry journals, books, and blogs; attend professional associations or conferences so that you're up to date with trends and industry information. And then find a way to measure your progress so that you don't get stuck. If, after a good try, getting hired in this industry looks like a bridge you can't cross, move on. Maybe it won't be your next job, but it could be the one after that. You always have to balance your financial needs with your strategy so that you have a good chance of finding work before your money runs out.

A WAY TO OPEN THE DOOR TO A NEW INDUSTRY

Lewis was in his late 20s and went right from college to working in financial services in New York City. He loved his job at a major bank and used his finance degree and MBA (which he got a few years later) to move into a business analyst role. Everything was great until the bank decided it needed to reduce expenses and Lewis's job, along with many others, was eliminated.

Aside from an addiction to his BlackBerry, he was easy to work with. Within two weeks his resume was done and he joined my weekly team. Like many people, he was hesitant about networking, but he was able to reach out to his friends and neighbors. Through them, he made some excellent connections. As I asked about

(continued)

(continued)

his goals, he told me that he wanted to get out of financial services and into the pharmaceutical industry. And because he lived in New Jersey where many large firms are located, he thought this would be fairly easy. It wasn't.

Even with help from his network, he kept getting the dreaded message: We prefer to hire candidates who have already worked in pharma. So he asked me what to do. I suggested trying employment agencies because they have strong relationships with companies and are often filling contract or temporary jobs.

"But I don't want a temporary job."

One of the most unpopular things I tell my clients when I hear this objection is, "All jobs are temporary." I tried this out on Lewis and he got a bit flustered.

"You know what I mean. I don't want to work for three months and then have to look for work again."

"I get that," I told him, "and I don't blame you. But if you're serious about break-ing into a new industry, I think it's something you should at least consider."

A few more weeks went by and the interview he'd had at one of the major phar-maceutical firms didn't result in an offer. He was now ready to try contract work. We put together a list of the employment agencies that are strong in that industry. He got his resume out to them, followed up, and was brought in by several for screening interviews. A month later he had a six-month contract. He had his foot in the door.

Several months into the job I happened to be coaching a client at this same firm, so we had lunch together. Lewis's contract had already been extended even though he wasn't at the end of his six months. He loved the job and now could update his resume and add that he had solid pharmaceutical experience.

Quick Do's and Don'ts

Do:

1. Carefully research both the industries and the companies you're interested in. If you don't know how to do this, ask for help from the reference librarian at your local library.

2. See if you can find a mentor in your target industry, or at least get advice from someone whose experience could help you.

3. Create a realistic timetable for your search and have a contingency plan so that if you need to earn some money while your search continues, you'll know how you're going to do it (see appendix D). In general, if you're going after a new industry or function, your search will take a bit longer.

4. See whether you can shadow someone in this new industry whose function is similar to yours to make sure you will like working in the industry. He or she may also offer advice to help you make this transition.

5. Look at the course offerings at a local community college. The fees are reasonable, and many of these institutions provide practical classes that could help you try a new industry. (And be sure to network with the professor.)

Don't:

1. Assume you know which industries will be interested in your background. With the right approach (a strong introduction, an employment agency, an internship, and so on), you might be surprised by the doors that will open.

2. Broadcast a negative message. It serves no purpose, and it will not only make you feel worse but will also shut down your network. (An example would be, "There are no jobs in the telecommunications industry.")

3. Focus on the details. Don't ignore the details, but looking at the big picture can help you see that you have transferable skills. Some companies intentionally look for new hires from other industries, so don't assume that lack of industry experience limits your chances.

Resources and Ideas

When I first started working in the outplacement industry, the company I worked for had an interesting grid that illustrated what might make a search easy and what would be considered a stretch. The two variables were function and industry, with the easiest search being the same—same function, same industry. The next level was to change one of the variables, so it would either be the same function in a new industry, or a new industry with the same function. And the biggest challenge (what we would predict as taking more time and possibly not working out at all) was when both function and industry were different. So if you'd been a programmer in the telecommunications industry but now wanted to be a project manager in consumer products, you had a steep mountain to climb. Here are resources to help you no matter which combination you choose:

- Professional associations are wonderful because most of them do a great job of providing complex industry information either through their meetings or their Web sites, directories, publications, and so on. In other words, if you want to make sure your function or skill set is up to date; if you're exploring a new, possibly related function in your own industry; or if you want to explore new industries, you really should look into associations. Plus, being part of these groups is fun. Job search can be lonely. As one of my clients said when I asked him what he had learned from his job search, "You gotta get out of the house!"

- Certifications are another way to go. If, for example, you are a project manager but haven't earned a certification, this might be the perfect time to add the PMP certification to your credentials.

- Read books about the industry you're targeting and write to the authors. Explain your situation and ask them for other resources and advice. Fan letters or e-mails are often answered.
- Use your list of companies in your search map to get feedback from people in the industry or industries you're targeting. Some companies are more open than others. By getting advice from those inside the industry, you'll have current information and new contacts that could help you make this transition.

CHAPTER 27

MYTH: I CAN'T GET A JOB BECAUSE ENGLISH IS NOT MY NATIVE LANGUAGE

I really admire people who conduct a job search in a language and culture that are not their own. It's hard enough in your own native tongue, but when you add all the idioms and cultural knowledge that are only picked up over time, it can create a serious challenge.

In a strong job market, especially in technical fields such as IT or science, this didn't matter so much. The recruiters or hiring managers were focused on credentials (work experience, education, and technical skills) and didn't care or seem to care that a candidate spoke with an accent. What I'm seeing now in my work with clients from many different countries is a different expectation. And because phone screenings are common in these areas, being understandable over the phone is critical.

With contingency recruiters who often conduct these screenings, their fees are contingent upon placement, and the job they're trying to fill is usually given to other firms as well. So they have to work fast and might not promote difficult-to-understand candidates to the employer because these candidates slow them down.

Here are some suggestions, and then we'll look at a specific example that illustrates how to minimize language issues. If you have a name that is difficult for Americans to pronounce (and from my experience, I believe that many Americans aren't very good with other languages), see if you can come up with initials or an American name that you add to your real name. So let's say you're from China and your first name is Chongwu. You could put the nickname "CJ" in parentheses after that, which might be easier to pronounce. Or let's say you're from India and your first name is Padmini. That's not difficult to say; but again, it reinforces your foreignness, so you could create a name like "Pam" and put that after your real first name in parentheses to indicate that it's a nickname.

Make sure you always say your name clearly and that your voice mail has an easy-to-understand message on it, only in English. If this creates a problem for family and friends who don't speak English, make your cell phone your job search phone and keep that voice-mail greeting professional and in English only. Also, speak slowly. It is much easier to understand someone if their pace is moderate. When you combine an accent and speed, it's much more difficult. And lastly, take away any discomfort the interviewer may have about understanding you.

Here's a sample phone script between a recruiter and a job seeker from India (we'll call him Prashant):

> **Recruiter:** Good morning. This is Jim from Get-a-Job Recruiting. We saw your resume on Indeed and wanted to talk to you about the Implementation Analyst position. Is this... (now there's an awkward pause because Jim doesn't know how to pronounce the candidate's name).
>
> **Prashant:** Yes, this is Prashant, but you but can call me PT—that's my nickname.
>
> **Recruiter:** Oh, that's easy. Thanks, PT. Before we get into the specific job, can you tell me why you were let go from your previous company?
>
> **Prashant:** I'd be glad to. Let me first mention that if you have any difficulty understanding me—English is my third language—please tell me and I'd be happy to repeat what I've said. I've never had any communication problems at work, but the phone can be a bit more challenging. Okay, what happened at my company is that we lost a major contract, and as a result, my position and hundreds of others were eliminated. That's why I'm excited about this opportunity because I have a strong background as an Implementation Analyst.
>
> **Recruiter:** Thanks. Now let me ask you some technical questions.

So what happened here is that PT made the recruiter comfortable and showed that he wasn't embarrassed by or worried about language issues. By putting it on the table, the issue went away. Now PT is a candidate who can be judged by the same criteria as the ones who are native English speakers. This levels the playing field.

WHEN PRIDE GETS IN THE WAY

Chang was from Taiwan. He came to the U.S. after graduating from college and attended graduate school in the Midwest. He was not the first in his extended family to come to the U.S., and he knew from his relatives, as well as his own experience, that this was where he had the best opportunities. He felt settled and secure in his job as a chemist at a major cosmetics firm. He loved the work and was regularly promoted. He and his wife and two children enjoyed a comfortable lifestyle in New Jersey. Then he lost his job.

I am not an expert on other cultures, but from what I've observed, this was a terrible blow to him because he believed that if he worked hard and was loyal, that he in essence "owned" his job. It was his. He might have realized that others could do the job, but that wasn't the point. He was good at it and there was no reason to worry about losing it. But he did.

Chang had a hard time in our initial weeks together. He looked embarrassed. He kept his head down when he spoke. But after his resume was done and he had attended some of our classes, he seemed to adjust. I kept telling him that he had an excellent background and that this process takes time. We talked about how it was important not to put all his effort into Internet postings, often discussing how to run a balanced search.

By posting his resume and reaching out to recruiters, he began to have phone screenings or interviews. This raised his hopes. He believed that his resume was doing its job—creating interest in his background. But after a few minutes on the phone, the recruiters would abruptly say "Thanks," or "I appreciate talking with you," and then they'd hang up. In other words, he wasn't getting past the phone screenings.

"Why is this happening?" he asked me.

"I'm not sure, but let's review both what you're saying and how you're saying it," I said.

He didn't mind going over the "what," but as I mentioned that they might be having a hard time understanding him—he had a heavy accent and spoke very quickly—he let me know there was no way he was going to tell recruiters that he was from Taiwan or that he'd be happy to repeat anything that they might not have understood.

A few more weeks went by and he went from embarrassed to deeply discouraged. Again I suggested that if he brought up the language issue, it might no longer be a liability. He shook his head and wouldn't do it. I reminded him that given our current tough job market, he was making it too easy for recruiters to dismiss him.

We explored other ways to expand his market, such as looking at temp or contract work. He was open to that. Through his network as well as using one of our databases, he found several firms that were strong in contract work for scientists. His phone was ringing again and I begged him to find some way—it didn't have to be my way—to get the language barrier out of the way. He did it, and quickly landed a three-month contract job, which then became permanent (or what I skeptically call "so-called permanent").

I can't prove that one thing led to another—that, because he was willing to put his communications issues up front, he got the job. But I can say I strongly believe it helped. Whenever there is a potential obstacle, it usually helps to address it.

Quick Do's and Don'ts

Do:

1. Get feedback on how you sound—both in person and over the phone. This is particularly important if English is not your first language. But even for native speakers, this is a good idea. Many people talk too fast or too softly to be understood completely.

2. Create a statement that will put others at ease—whether it's like the one we looked at earlier or perhaps one that explains a disability. Because I learned

American Sign Language several years ago, I work with most of our deaf or hearing-impaired clients. E-mail and instant messaging have vastly improved communications, but if you have a hearing loss, you have to explain why talking on the phone (except through a relay service) isn't your best way to go.

3. Create a name, nickname, or initials that are easy for native speakers to pronounce.

4. Make sure you include your citizenship or green card status on your resume so that if your name makes people think that you're not from the U.S., you can put any legal concerns to rest.

Don't:

1. Assume that your technical knowledge, education, publications, patents, and so on will sell you by themselves. You are going to have to talk to people (or find other ways to communicate if talking isn't possible) as part of the search process.

2. Speak quickly. This often compounds other issues such as speaking with an unfamiliar accent. (And within this huge country, we all know there are a lot of different accents and idioms, so that a person from Texas might wonder what someone from Maine is saying.)

3. Stick stubbornly to a strategy that isn't working. Brainstorm with a career counselor or someone you trust, and analyze what's not working and why.

Resources and Ideas

*   Join Toastmasters or any organization that gives you the chance to make presentations and receive helpful feedback.

*   Enroll in a Dale Carnegie course or a public speaking course at your local community college. This will not only give you good practice, but it will also help you expand your network.

*   Hire a language coach. There are people who specialize in accent reduction using workbooks, audio reinforcement, and a highly effective system. See if this might be a good investment. (You can find the one that I've used at www.languagedirections.com.)

*   Have someone take video of you answering interview questions. As you listen to the video, pay attention to language and accent issues.

*   Anything you can do to strengthen your ability to communicate effectively is a wonderful investment during your job search campaign that will pay off.

CHAPTER 28

MYTH: THE INTERNET IS THE FASTEST WAY TO GET A JOB

This may be one of the most difficult myths to shake. I estimate that at least 70 percent or more of my clients (past, present, or to come) are hooked on this one. Only after intense discouragement will they give it up. So although I've touched on how hiring happens and why it's a good idea to balance your search so that you're using a wide range of techniques (and hopefully beating out the competition), this one bears looking at a little more closely.

To set the record straight, I love the Internet. It's amazing how quickly you can research anything from what your old car is worth to the best vegetarian restaurant in Toledo. Pre-Internet there were the want ads, but the process of applying to jobs was more cumbersome. So now you've got this nifty and fast way of seeing what companies want and sending in your resume. But the big problem is volume, and this is compounded by the resume sorting process.

First there's the problem of volume. If you see an ad for an operations manager on Monster, Indeed, CareerBuilder, or wherever, so do hundreds if not thousands of other operations managers. So by the time a position is posted, it's really too late. (This is not always the case, which is why most career counselors will tell you to include Internet job searching along with other efforts.)

Second, whose job is it to sort through the avalanche of resumes to pick the ones that go into the yes, no, and maybe piles? Usually it's human resources (HR). So if your background is a bit different, or if you happen to be in the part of the pile that never even gets looked at, you're out of luck. And if this job is a stretch for you in any way, forget it. To be really perverse about this, if you want to experience a high and consistent level of rejection, focus solely on Internet ads and pick postings where you're not a great match. The rule of thumb is that you should meet 85 to 90 percent of the requirements before even thinking about responding to the ad.

Let's say you see an ad and you match only about 60 percent of what they're looking for. But you're really interested in the company because it's growing, it makes a product you love, it's close to where you live, or you've heard great things about it. In addition to answering the ad (and some would say instead of answering the ad), figure out a way to get inside information and hopefully get to the decision maker or hiring manager. LinkedIn is an easy way to see whether you know someone who knows someone at the company. Making sure you ask your overall network is another way. And if that fails, going directly to the hiring manager or targeting is a third choice. I mentioned how to do this in chapter 21 and there's a sample template in appendix B.

So back to the myth. Why is it so powerful and persistent? Here's my theory: Responding to Internet ads makes you feel productive. It's certainly easy to get sucked into the feeling that this is a real job and that anyone with a brain will see that you're a match and should call you within five minutes. But this doesn't happen. So like the news, I tell my clients that they're on an Internet diet as well. And if they're having a hard time limiting their online surfing, then I suggest a daily schedule that gives them specific times to use the Internet: for research, answering ads, posting their resumes, and so on. Just please make sure *you're* using *it,* and not the other way around.

THE INTERNET ADDICTION

Julia didn't believe in networking, didn't know how to do it, and was in IT, so she was really happy on her computer. She was tech savvy and was convinced that her background would sell itself. It did the last time, so why should she change? Why should she listen to what we were suggesting through our manual, classes, and counseling sessions?

When I hit this level of resistance, I try to explain that what we in the outplacement and career counseling field know a lot about is the hiring process—or how to look for a job. We're not trying to prove that we're right, but we are focused on how to help people through a tricky process. Our goal is always to get our clients to good offers as quickly as possible.

Because I knew that Julia wouldn't talk to people, or at least not yet, I suggested she use e-mail as a way to reach out to her connections. I got a dull stare and a shake of the head.

"It's not their job," she said quietly.

"You're right," I told her, "but I think it is your job to help other people help you."

"I don't want to bother them. They're busy with their own lives."

"Right again. We all are. But if you do the groundwork, if you come up with a plan for your search that includes a list of companies you're interested in, then you wouldn't be burdening others by simply asking if they could take a few moments to look at the list."

"I'd rather answer ads."

I laughed because I was relieved that she was so honest. "Sure you would—it's easier (at least at first). And when you hit the Send button, you feel as if you've really accomplished something. But tell me what has happened so far from the ones you've answered?"

She looked down at the table and wouldn't reply.

"All I'm saying, Julia, is think of yourself as a scientist or an explorer. You're in foreign territory and you've got a really important goal: finding your next job. You don't have to give up applying to ads online. I'm simply suggesting you add some other efforts to the mix."

I realized that I was in lecture mode, which is what I slip into when I get upset, so I took a deep breath and suggested we plan out what she might do for the next few days. I asked her if that was okay and she nodded. I understood she wasn't ready to change her tactics just yet, but I was hoping that if she had a plan in place, she might just try it.

Quick Do's and Don'ts

Do:

1. Take advantage of the wonderful resources you can find online. Use the Internet to research companies, connect with others, post your resume, find professional associations and recruiters, and answer ads.

2. Create a plan and a schedule so that your whole effort isn't spent online. There's too much competition and it's impersonal—two strikes against you.

3. Ask others (whether or not they're in transition) how they found their jobs. This is a wonderful way to educate yourself and to lay the groundwork for networking. (If you ask me how I found my current job, we're now talking about a topic that's critical for you if you're looking for work. Nine times out of ten, my response will be to ask you what you're looking for and how I can help.)

Don't:

1. Get seduced by the wealth of jobs posted online. Knowing what's out there is really smart, but limiting your efforts to answering ads often produces a long and frustrating search.

2. Keep doing something if it's not working. I spent a year chasing after agents to get this book published. One day it occurred to me that I had to change tactics because a whole year and 70 attempts were sending me a clear message. Once I focused on publishers instead of agents, I had an offer within two weeks.

3. Assume you know how you're going to get your next job. It's a quirky process where timing and luck factor in. I tell my clients that I don't know how they're going to get their next job but I do know how to help them run a really productive and effective search.

Resources and Ideas

If you're still having trouble diversifying your search, what can you do?

- Keep a careful log of your time and what you're doing with it. Put next to each entry what results you're getting. So if on a particular day in your search you answer six ads, keep track of whether you get any responses from them.

- Ask another job seeker who is getting interviews how he or she did it. This doesn't mean that if you do what they have done you'll achieve the same results, but finding out how others are getting to hiring managers is always helpful.

- Create and follow your daily schedule. If it's helpful, use the librarian trick of setting a kitchen timer to 10 minutes when you start an Internet search. When the buzzer goes off, you must have a clear sense of what you've found and how you'll use it to continue. Otherwise, log off or start a new search.

- Ask a search buddy to give you quotas to fulfill. If you commit to making three networking calls a day, that means that by the end of the week you should have reached out to 15 people. This method can help you stay accountable.

- Commit to getting out of the house at least once a day, preferably to attend a meeting, job fair, or conference where you'll have the chance to interact with other people. This will also get you away from your computer.

CHAPTER 29

IN HIS OWN WORDS: COURAGE AND PERSISTENCE

My journey began one fateful day in August 2008. After 24 years in the same location, and having survived three ownership changes, my job came to a screeching halt. It happened soon after the last change, as a result of the company's need to restructure its finances. The good news (to me, at least) was that I was not alone; I was part of a 10 percent reduction in force. Also good news, the job market was still humming…for about another month.

I began my search with all the energy and excitement I could muster. I made a list of just about everyone I knew and began organizing my records and setting up tracking spreadsheets. I got my resume together, circulated it to a few helpful critics, and started identifying target companies. I posted my resume on a few job boards and got a few early hits. One such hit was a near-perfect job opportunity with a company in Oklahoma City. After an initial phone screen, I was invited to meet the president of the company and the chairman of the board. They wanted me to join them. But for a guy from the East Coast, who had lived his entire life between New York City and Philadelphia, I couldn't commit, and the job fell through.

Then the job *market* fell through.

I redoubled my efforts, posted on more job boards, identified more companies, attended more networking events, and talked to more people. But companies just weren't hiring. I tried the consulting route but couldn't make much headway. There was too much competition and so much desperation that hourly rates were in the basement. I even hooked up with a couple of different groups and explored the possibility of starting up a new company, but the uncertainty of the times turned those prospects into pipedreams. I explored the possibility of buying a franchise, but dismissed it fairly quickly when I learned the magnitude of the financial commitment I was expected to make.

Several times during my extended period of vocational detachment, things seemed to turn around. All of a sudden, there'd be a flurry of activity. But like flurries, the opportunities seemed to melt and evaporate as soon as they hit the ground. Nevertheless, these respites of positive activity have kept me going and have buoyed my optimism.

I've applied for a lot of positions and had a reasonable number of phone and face-to-face interviews. But what I've found is that I'm primarily applying for the same positions as everyone else, and the competition is fierce. It's an employer's job market right now, and they're being very selective. So in the competitive arena, it's important to be as close a fit to the job description as possible, differentiate yourself from the competition, and be as compatible with their culture as you can be.

What's intuitively obvious, but obviously elusive, is finding unadvertised positions. For those, the competition will be limited or nonexistent. The best way to find such opportunities is through networking, which for many of us is akin to dental extraction. By networking, you might just stumble across someone who knows someone who needs someone, but hasn't really formalized a position just yet. Having a discussion with that someone may help them to write a job description around exactly what you have to offer.

Aside from my job search and my meager attempts at networking, I've been doing a lot of volunteer work. I also set up a support group for fellow executives whose outplacement services have expired, or as I like to put it, those who have been laid off from outplacement. We've helped each other considerably with connections, information, discussion, and moral support. Helping others takes a bit of pressure off the job search and even opens up opportunities for networking.

In the time I've been searching, I've been able to do several things that I probably would not have had time for if I was working. By authoring several op-eds for newspapers and other publications, I've been able to develop a dormant skill (writing) into something I might be able do something with in the future. I dealt with a medical situation that, unchecked, would have ended more than my career. I also dealt with the loss of two close family members, and was able to help them in their transitions and support the rest of the family after their passing. On the professional side, I took a couple of courses to prepare for a professional certification and became active in an industry association.

I was also fortunate to have paid off my mortgage, and to have graduated my youngest son from college. These two events significantly reduced my burn rate and made the loss of income much less painful. Extensions of unemployment programs have also helped, but the filing requirements can be a little onerous if you report any income but unemployment. Several of my colleagues who took on short-term assignments found their benefits cut off and had to spend many hours to get them restored.

Right now, I have about a half-dozen irons in the fire—I just can't tell whether the fire is lit. I intend to keep moving forward and feeding the network as much as I can. I'll also continue to do volunteer work and help others. It's one certain way to reward your own best efforts in a difficult time.

Robert P. Morgan, P.E.

PART 3

TURNING THE CORNER, OR
THE WAY FORWARD

CHAPTER 30

HOW TO MAKE ENVY PRODUCTIVE

Envy is one of those emotions you're not supposed to have. Many people consider it rude or weak, but I like to think of it as an indicator—as something that might help you determine what's important to you. And isn't it interesting that envy is often associated with the color green, just like jealousy? Of course, full-blown envy isn't helpful because it's usually a trap. But now that you hopefully have a strong foundation for your job search—and like Diane, whose story is at the end of part 1, you're able to recognize that your value hasn't changed—it might be useful to think a bit about envy. Who do you wish you were? Who do you admire?

In this exercise you could aim high and dream about being Oprah or a highly recognized sports figure. Or maybe someone in politics or an inventor, scientist, or artist is your ideal. Aside from the obvious differences between you and them (your envy may really spike when you realize that they don't have to look for a new job), think about what you most admire about them and ways that you can take a step in that direction.

Sticking with Oprah for a moment, some may admire her for coming such a long way from her poor, rural childhood, while others might be more impressed with the ways she empowers other women. Make a list of the things that impress you and see whether you can find out how this person accomplished what he or she did. Most importantly, you want to look at what drove this person—what got him or her through hardship and discouragement.

Here's another way to look at this. I think it's sometimes easier to change from the outside in. George Washington is said to have studied how the British military demonstrated rank. Because he believed that it was important to look like a leader, he designed a blue and buff uniform with metal buttons that made him look like a general. He knew that his image, as well as many other qualities including his experience and his leadership abilities, could either work for him or against him. One of his uniforms can be seen at the Smithsonian Institution (although not ones from during the Revolution), and blue and buff remained the army uniform colors until the Civil War. So think about how you look and see if you can get your image to support your goals. This doesn't mean that you now must be one of the beautiful people we see on TV or in magazines, but it does mean that if you're a strong manager with a track record of motivating your staff, you need to look the part.

Several years ago, when I would go clothes shopping, I'd tell myself to look for "successful author outfits." I didn't feel like a successful author. But I knew that if I started to look like one, it could help. As discussed earlier in this book, get feedback from someone whose advice you value, and be willing to experiment with the impression you make. This is change from the outside in.

One of the key components of change is awareness (for example, if you're dieting, you need to first be aware of what you're eating, when you're eating it, and perhaps even how). So as you pay attention to your daydreams, see who you admire or envy. See what groups you feel you really belong to. I have a new client who I invited to attend a meeting of the Association of Career Professionals because she had expressed an interest in career counseling. After the meeting she told me, "I felt I belonged there. I was comfortable but also really jazzed up." This is a strong sign that this might be a good direction for her to pursue.

What many of my clients experience is envy of anyone who is working, no matter what their position, because it's easy to feel that you'll never work again. Even when you observe someone who has a job you don't want, you feel envious because at least that other person doesn't have to go through this terrible process. In my first job in the outplacement industry, one of my colleagues used to tell senior executives that if they wanted a job, they could get one within the day. He then told them that the gas station around the corner had a "help wanted" sign. Before the group turned on him, he explained the difference between finding any job and a professional search. His point was that they were managing a complex process that was going to take effort and time.

When my clients are struggling with envy or are just plain stuck, I remind them that they do have a job—which is looking for a new opportunity—and that they will work again. I also point out that one of the advantages of this job is that you're the boss—you're determining your goals, your implementation strategy, and your schedule. That means you have some flexibility and can help friends or family members who may need you during this time, or you can learn something new, or give yourself interesting breaks and visit the local museum or park that you've never had time to explore. The key here is what you do with envy and making sure that you allow yourself only small doses.

Too much envy leads to resentment and paralysis. And sometimes when we envy someone, we're not interested in the effort and time it took them to get where they are, but simply want to be magically transformed into them. That's not going to happen, so make sure that as you think about the people you admire, you understand how they got where they are—what small steps and persistence got them from one day to the next. It's the culmination of small efforts that usually leads to big changes.

WORK TO LIVE OR LIVE TO WORK

This doesn't happen often, but the first time a client said to me, "I want to be you," I nearly fell off my chair.

"What?"

"You have a part-time schedule, you enjoy your work, you balance that with your own projects (writing), and you play tennis, so how bad could that be?"

"Not bad at all," I said, smiling, "but you need to be you, not me."

As we discussed this further, what surfaced was that my client had realized that it was possible to have a different relationship with work. Work is important (both financially and in terms of feeling useful), but it doesn't have to eclipse everything else—and with a different balance there can be time for friendship, children, pets, hobbies, and yourself. This diversity of interests also serves to prevent burnout. If things are tough at work, you can focus on other aspects of your life.

And lastly, one thing feeds another. Using my own schedule as an example, I'll write in the mornings and then garden in the afternoon, or I'll see clients all day and then take my dog to agility training at night. What I've learned from my recreational or release activities has helped me become a better counselor and writer because both gardening and dog training prove that patience pays off. And they're fun.

So when Heather, who had decided to make a radical change in her work-life balance, mentioned that she envied me, I burst out laughing and told her that my compensation was nowhere near her six-figure salary.

"I know," she said, "but since my former company has made it clear that they don't want me anymore, and since I've got severance, unemployment, and services with you, shouldn't I do something I've always dreamed of doing?"

"Yes," I told her, "as long as you can meet your financial needs and have the drive or stamina it takes to make it happen. It's really discouraging to go after something and fail, so I think it's smart to do some careful planning."

"But Jean, we've worked on my resume together. You know what kind of analysis and planning I've done in the past. Don't you think I can pull this off?"

"No doubt about it, but let's work on a plan with a timeline so that you have a way to measure how you're doing. And let's also think of some ways you can road-test your ideas before you implement them to make sure they're going to work."

A quick note on the concept of road-testing your ideas: Other people love to give advice, and this is a wonderful way to engage others and motivate them to help you. You tell them your idea or concept for your business or your job search and you ask for feedback. And it's really smart to get diverse points of view so that, for example, you're tapping into a consultant's perspective, a finance person's expertise, and so on.

(continued)

(continued)

Heather agreed, created her plan with a timeline, and shared it with others. A month later she had started consulting for a friend's business and had also set up a series of seminars that formed the foundation for her own venture. She was well on her way to work that was satisfying in itself, but that would also allow her time with her children—a personal priority. She was creating her own work schedule. Although there were risks (because consulting can be unpredictable), she had given herself the chance to explore this radically new way of balancing life and work.

Quick Do's and Don'ts

Do:

1. Look at envy as a helpful tool. Make a list of people you admire and why and then find out how they accomplished what they did. These don't have to be well-known people. You might have a neighbor who is really special—learn more about him or her.

2. Realize that most accomplishments are the result of a lot of little steps. See what small thing you can do today (this might be something you've been avoiding) that will help your search move forward.

3. Allow yourself balance activities. For some this might be sitting quietly and reading the newspaper, whereas for others it might be an active project where you build or make something.

Don't:

1. Let envy paralyze you. A small amount can be motivating, but large doses are unproductive. At the heart of a healthy relationship with envy is acceptance of yourself. When I coach my clients in preparation for interviews, I always stress that they need to be themselves. That doesn't mean that they can necessarily do what feels natural or comfortable if their presentation skills need improving, but it does mean that one of their key goals is revealing who they are, how they think, what motivates them, and so on.

2. Compare yourself with others who are also in the search process. Here's an example: A client says to me, "Why did she land a job? I'm twice as talented and have way more experience. I just don't get it!" This is not the good kind of envy because it pits you against another job seeker. It's particularly unproductive because we don't know what the company who hired this person wanted. Be happy for others when they land their new jobs, stay connected to them, learn from them, and your turn will come.

3. Wish to be someone else. Who you are—your personal history, work experience, education, attributes, outside interests, and so on—give you a unique perspective. And that's a key part of what you're "selling." And, sure, all of us can improve, but we've also got to be comfortable with who we are.

Resources and Ideas

Julia Cameron, in her wonderful book, *The Artist's Way,* reveals envy or jealousy for what it is: "a mask for fear." And she goes on to say that "jealousy is a stingy emotion. It doesn't allow for the abundance and multiplicity of the universe." So if you feel afraid, if you're waking up at night wondering how you'll pay the mortgage and are convinced you'll never work again, ask yourself these questions:

- Do I have a budget so that I know how long I can go without income?
- What's my plan B that I'll implement if my search goes on longer than expected?
- How have I used my time so far in my search? Am I running a well-balanced and productive search, or am I addicted to one method whether or not it's working?
- Am I maximizing the contacts I have? Who could really help me? (This can include people you know as well as ones you don't but who could be very helpful because of their backgrounds, industry knowledge, connections, and so on.)
- What am I doing to keep myself energized and positive? (A breakfast date is an inexpensive way to get out of the house and do something fun with a spouse or friend.)
- How am I helping others?
- Am I making good use of LinkedIn and other social media to create an online presence? (Facebook, Twitter, and Plaxo are other resources.)

CHAPTER 31

PREPARE FOR INTERVIEW SURPRISES

My team gave me a wonderful phrase as we were talking about being close to getting an offer—but before it was in the bag: "Nothing is anything until it's something."

I had to repeat it several times before I got it, but I think it conveys the slippery part of the job search process when you're getting close. And close is good, it's encouraging, but it isn't time yet to let down your guard or heave a huge sigh of relief.

I don't think this phrase means you have to become paranoid and not trust anyone or any part of this complicated process, but I do think it's a good reminder to protect yourself. It forces you to remember that a lot of things can happen that you have no control over, which could include a sudden hiring freeze, a change in leadership, an acquisition, outsourcing, political change, natural disasters, and so on. Like a runner who can't slow down when he or she sees the finish line, you've got to keep going full steam ahead until your offer is signed, sealed, and delivered.

What complicates this advice is that interviewing takes an awful lot of time and energy. You've got to conduct careful research on the company as well as on the individuals who will be interviewing you. You need in many ways to be single-minded—selecting your accomplishment stories and practicing them so that you're well prepared. You have to anticipate what the company might ask you as well as needs that aren't part of the job description. And it's never a bad idea to do a practice run so that you won't get lost when you go in for an interview—which is another time commitment.

Some of my clients confess that they have gone on interviews where they've "winged it." This is not a good idea, even if you're pretty sure this is a job you don't want. That kind of experience tends to bring you down rather than build you up. So as a professional, whether you work on an assembly line or are Chief Financial Officer, you are going to be well prepared for all your interviews.

One of the tools I like to give my clients is what I call the "interview map." This is basically a cheat sheet with the name of the company on the top, followed by the name and title of the interviewer (you'll make a separate sheet or map for each person you're meeting with). Underneath this you create two columns: On the left you put a list of the job responsibilities as you know them from the published job description, the recruiter, your research, and what you can learn from inside contacts. On the right you put keywords to remind yourself of your credentials and accomplishments. So let's say you initiated a program at your last company that reduced expenses by 37 percent. You might have to put only the number in the right column as a reminder of the whole story.

After the two columns, you write down your prepared questions for them—usually about three. These could be specific to the role, for example, "Will the person you hire also be responsible for generating new business?" or they could be more general questions that show you're motivated and a good problem solver. An example might be, "What's the biggest challenge facing your new (add the title here)?" Even if you decide that you don't need to refer to this map during the interview, the fact that you've thought through what the company is looking for and how you match will give you a competitive edge.

So now let's look at the interview itself and how you might use this two-column cheat sheet. If the industry is one where information is sensitive or confidential, you need to ask whether it's alright to take notes. If that's not the case, do whatever makes you more comfortable. I usually don't ask because I believe that note taking is a good way to show interest and attention and it makes me look as if I'm already working for the company. An additional benefit is that it gives me a natural way to break eye contact, so while the interviewer is talking, I can glance down at my map, jot down a word or two, and then look back up. This is a whole lot better than a staring contest, which is guaranteed to make both sides uncomfortable.

Another advantage of having and using this two-column list is that you can keep track of what you've discussed and which stories you've shared. If you're being interviewed by only two or three people, this isn't usually a problem. But if it's one of those all-day affairs (I call this the meat-grinder interview), you need a way to keep a careful accounting of what you've said to whom. And lastly, when you write your thank-you e-mails after the interview, your notes will help you tailor them, so that you're covering the issues of most importance for each person.

HIRED AND UNHIRED AT THE SAME TIME

Kathleen had worked for major food manufacturers her whole career. She had risen to a senior sales management position and loved her work. As we discussed her goals, she made it clear that she had no interest in anything but this industry. As she created her list of potential employers or target companies, she realized that she would have to expand beyond her local area—central New Jersey—in order to have enough chances.

At about the three-month mark in her search, she began interviewing, first with a local company and then with one of her top choices in the Midwest. Both

(continued)

(continued)

interviews went really well and she used her strong network to get inside information and to have people who were known to the hiring managers recommend her.

She was on my team, so she was aware of the "nothing is anything until it's something" mantra, and was careful with her expectations. She reached out to a few new recruiters and started researching the next company on her list. A week or so later the company in the Midwest called her back for a second round of interviews. Things went so well that the HR representative hooked her up with a real-estate agent so that she could get a sense of the housing market while she was out there. When we met again, she was really excited.

"This is the job I want," she told me, "and it's as if they're tailoring it to my exact background."

"That's great," I said "but what's their time frame—when will they be making an offer?"

"HR said I'll get a letter this week. Through the recruiter we had already worked out salary, so aside from a few small issues and my start date, we're good to go."

Now I felt like a wet blanket. "That's very good and I hope it all happens as planned. But just to be on the safe side, can you continue with your other efforts?"

She rolled her eyes at me. "If I have to."

"Yup, you do."

The letter arrived, we reviewed it at our next meeting, and Kathleen had a start date with only three weeks to find a new home. The company paid for her to fly out again and she spent two exhausting days looking at condos and single-family homes. She also had to prepare her condo in New Jersey for sale—a huge job—although she thought she might rent it instead to give herself more time. She brought donuts to our next team meeting and we celebrated her wonderful success. End of story, right? Not exactly.

Two weeks later as she was frantically working on her real-estate issues, she received a call. The company rescinded the offer. She called me in full panic.

"Jean, what does this mean?"

I asked for the details and listened carefully. I was as stunned as she was.

"Did they give any reasons?" I asked.

"No, just that they looked at their overall business plan and decided to pull the plug."

We talked for a while more and I did my best to reassure her that this had nothing to do with her. It couldn't have. But something had happened and neither she nor I knew what it was. The only good thing we could find in all of this was that she hadn't put her condo on the market, but still it was a terrible blow. Kathleen worried about coming back to the team. I told her to take a week off if she wanted, but not to feel embarrassed. Then the strangest thing happened: When she gave her report at the team meeting two weeks later, she had a smile on her face.

"Well," she told us, "I'm happy to say that I just received my first paycheck."

"What?" I asked.

"This wonderful company that hired me, and then very quickly unhired me, obviously doesn't know which end is up. I've got my first paycheck and I'm really tempted to cash it."

Two weeks later she received a second check. By now Kathleen had moved on and wasn't as upset, so she e-mailed HR and asked them what they'd like her to do with these checks because she wasn't an employee. She was asked to return them and did. Fast-forward two months: She accepted a better offer with a local company and had learned from this wild experience that the team mantra was spot on.

Quick Do's and Don'ts

Do:

1. Prepare thoroughly for interviews and be "cautiously optimistic." As mentioned earlier, aim for the middle—not wildly up or depressingly down. In the interview process, your job is to be well prepared, to listen carefully, and to present yourself with strong accomplishment examples.

2. Recognize the difference between what you can control and what you can't. And reward yourself for each milestone, whether it's an interview well done, a good networking meeting, or simply making a call that you didn't want to make.

3. Maintain momentum. Stopping in the search process for more than a short break usually makes it much harder to get back to a strong level of productivity. Work your map or plan, stick to your schedule, and you'll get there.

Don't:

1. Stop. Don't let encouraging signs lull you into inactivity. It's good that things are happening, but use that positive energy to invest in new leads. It isn't over until you have a written offer. (Kathleen's story is a very rare case of when it wasn't even over then.)

2. Tell others that you have an offer until all the details are worked out. It's really hard to go back to your network and tell them that this sure thing fell through. A client I'm currently working with thought he had an offer with a company in Michigan where he and his family used to live. His wife told all their friends that they would be moving back to the Midwest, and then the offer fell through. This knocked the wind out of his sails and made it very hard for him to start up his search again.

3. Let the things you can't control discourage you. Okay, let them bother you for a little while and then get back to work. You have a really important job, which is finding a job, and it's smart to learn what you can from the ups and downs that are an inevitable part of this process.

Resources and Ideas

A course that I designed and teach at work is called "Interview Techniques That Could Save Your Life." In it I cover the two-column map described earlier and also look at two other skills: probing and pitching (more on these in chapter 36). The resource I want to share with you here is ways to use this map. And although it can't prevent the ups and downs of the hiring process, it gives you structure and clear goals.

- Prepare your map and review it carefully before an interview.
- Open your portfolio or folder during the interview and refer to your map.
- Take notes on your map so that your follow-up e-mails are tailored to the individual interviewer's needs.
- Make copies of your map for each person you're meeting with and put them in a folder with a copy of your resume and your business card. If you want to make this more tailored, put the name and title of the person on the cover of the folder along with the company name. Give this to them during the interview so that they can see you're a great match.
- If you have an inside contact at the company where you're interviewing, ask them for information so that your map will be even more focused on the company's needs.
- If you're seeing only a few people and you don't feel that nervous, try this technique: Prepare your map, look at it just before you go on the interview, but don't refer to it.
- When the interview is over, take a few minutes, in your car or in the lobby of the building, to jot down what you did well and what you wish you had done differently. This might include an accomplishment story that you wish you had told one of the interviewers. Don't let that bother you—it almost always happens and you can include it in your thank-you e-mail.
- Remember that many interviewers aren't well trained and often don't like interviewing. And some may be just as nervous as you are. Focus on their needs, listen carefully, follow your map, and you'll be fine.

CHAPTER 32

USE TRANSITION AS AN OPPORTUNITY

From the examples you've read so far in this book, you should have a good sense of how other people have taken advantage of an involuntary break from work. This doesn't mean they didn't have a difficult time or have days when they wondered whether they'd ever work again. But it does show that there is life beyond job loss and that many have used this time to find better jobs or to make significant changes. How do you get yourself turned around so that loss can become opportunity?

As Ken Paul's story illustrates at the end of this part, you're going to have to find your way through this. As he put it, "So I went about my search doing my best to discount the half-truths and avoid the obstacles." In other words, you're in charge, you have your map or plan as well as your daily schedule, and like a detective or an explorer, you're following clues and putting together the pieces. You try things and evaluate what happens. You talk with others to see what they think. You look at where you're getting traction and where nothing is happening. You monitor your results and get better at this as you go.

This doesn't mean that you ignore the advice of career professionals. Our advantage is that we know a lot about what makes a search effective. We get to be part of hundreds of searches a year, so we accumulate extensive data to support this. What I'm trying to say here is that it's really helpful if you have an open mind and are willing to try things—even things that may feel a bit uncomfortable at first.

So here you are, with your job gone, and perhaps you're clarifying not only what you want, but also how you're going to get there. You have the materials to support your search: a strong resume, a business card (see appendix E), your references, and a growing network on LinkedIn. You're getting more comfortable talking about yourself. You can explain why you're no longer with your company without hesitating, you can give specific examples of how you made a difference at your past job or jobs, and you can answer the "why should I hire you?" question effectively—articulating your competitive advantage. (There's more on this in chapter 36.)

As you define your goals and determine your timeline (this means how much time you have before you need income beyond severance and unemployment compensation), you may want to think about what work you really enjoyed and what your next opportunity might look like. If, for example, you've been managing a large staff and are good at it but don't really enjoy it, this could be a time to explore getting back to an individual contributor role. Or, let's say you always envied the consultants your former company hired because they seemed to really enjoy their work and were usually able to steer clear of office politics. This could be a good time to talk to some consultants and consulting firms to see what that kind of work would be like.

Some career changes are subtle but meaningful nonetheless. You could end up in the same role in the same industry but go from a large company to a small one. Or your new opportunity might offer you a chance to work from home—an option many find attractive. As I work with clients who want to make significant changes, we often use the Myers-Briggs Type Indicator and the Strong Interest Inventory to give them additional ways to understand themselves and to see the occupations of those with a similar type or interests.

I currently have several clients exploring buying franchises. For a few of them, I suspect this is something that they'll do in the next month or two once they've completed their research and have figured out the financing. For some of the others, I believe this won't become the next job for them, but very well may be the one after that. In other words, they're using this break from work to begin doing the groundwork for future opportunities. This is wonderful because they realize that their next job serves as a bridge to their ultimate goal, buying them time during which they can create a strong foundation for this next, very important step.

BABY BOOMER MENTALITY

Aaron was a Vietnam War veteran in his early 60s with an in-depth knowledge of the insurance industry. Right out of the military he landed his first job in this industry and had been in it his entire career. He was a strong manager and also had extensive technical expertise. He worked hard and had a great sense of humor, which made him popular at work. He had risen up through the ranks and earned a base of $150,000 with a 20 percent bonus.

The first thing I noticed about Aaron was that he wasn't bitter; he was a highly independent person. He did, however, think that his former company had made a huge strategic mistake, but he quickly understood that this wasn't his problem. In the first few weeks of his transition, he couldn't truly separate from his company because both his direct reports and other managers at his level kept calling him. They wanted to know how he was doing and to offer help, but also kept talking about why this had happened—which no one could explain.

So the first thing we worked on was how he was going to protect himself from these conversations. I suggested a script that might go something like, "Thanks very much for calling me. I really appreciate it and as I put together my search plan, I'll be getting back in touch with you to get your advice. I don't mean this to sound rude, but what would really help right now is not talking about my former company because that makes it harder for me to move ahead. Is that okay?"

Aaron laughed. "You make that sound so easy."

"It's not," I agreed, "but some way or another, you've got to get uninvolved with the issues at work, right?"

He nodded.

When I asked Aaron how he was using his time, he told me that he was working on a range of ideas about what he might want to do next, but that he was also having fun. He played golf with friends, went out to dinner with his wife, and was taking a course to keep his industry knowledge current.

At about the two-month mark, Aaron decided to take advantage of our entrepreneurial resources. He thought he might want to set up his own consulting firm. He had a close friend who was still employed by his former company, and together they had just the right combination of expertise to capture new business. He worked through his business plan, had a Web site created, set up an LLC, and began contacting potential customers.

A month or so later, he came to our meeting with a huge smile on his face and told me that he was working again. Without violating his non-compete agreement with his former company, he and his partner had won their first assignment. And he loved it. It was work, it drew on his extensive experience, but now he was the boss. And because of the flexibility of consulting, he saw himself working for at least another decade. (This is an area where very often age is considered an asset.)

Before Aaron and I wrapped up his program, he reminded me that he had been unsure at the beginning whether he would be good at prospecting and it was still a concern because he knew he couldn't stop looking for new business. But with each contract he was getting better at it; plus, he had testimonials from his clients that would give potential clients a way to see how his services had made a difference. He told me that he never would have walked away from his former company, but now he was glad they had let him go because he had found work that was a great fit. We laughed about being baby boomers and how we were changing the rules for retirement, as we had for so many other things. He sure had no intention of sitting in a rocking chair all day.

Quick Do's and Don'ts

Do:

1. Use this involuntary break from work to do some career planning. You may be very good at the work you've done so far, but take a little time to consider whether this is what you'd like to continue doing.

2. Take advantage of resources that can help you with career planning. This might include an outplacement program, a local job search group, the PSG

or Professional Services Group at the One-Stop career centers, or books such as *What Color Is Your Parachute?* (or other books that are specific to a career you're exploring).

3. Make an immediate and longer-term plan, balancing your interests with your financial needs. Some clients I have worked with have a year's severance pay, so they can afford to take more time than someone who has only a few weeks.

Don't:

1. Jump back into work that you've outgrown. It's often easier to get hired to do the exact same things you've just done, but create a plan that will get you into roles or industries that are of interest to you.

2. Assume you're stuck if you haven't even tried to find out what else is out there.

3. Decide that in this economy you have no choices. Make a realistic plan but don't rule out possibilities before you've explored them. At the depth of the financial crisis, many of the clients I worked with landed new jobs—some in the same function and industry and others that were quite different.

4. Take any job you can get just to avoid the uncertainty and effort of looking for work. This rarely leads to work you can sustain.

Resources and Ideas

• To recap, look carefully at how much time you have before you need a paycheck and benefits and see whether you can use this break to do some career planning. Ask others to help you make a list of what you do best and look at that list every day. Then see what roles or functions would allow you to use your particular skill set. If, for example, you're really good at mentoring others, you might be good in HR, could be a manager, or perhaps could explore training or teaching.

• Networking, when changing careers, goes from important to essential. You need others' help if you want to do something different. As you're looking at some new ways to work, make sure you're involving others because their feedback and connections will be critical. And go into this with the expectation that there will be days when you feel you're floundering and will never make it to a new job. That's just part of the process. You can't let those feelings stop you from moving forward. When my clients tell me they're out of work, I tell them that they now have a full-time job, which is finding a new opportunity. It's demanding, challenging, and full of ups and downs, but the result will be worth it.

- From my experience, most people won't leave jobs they hate. It's just too hard. But when a company makes this decision for you and lets you go, you now have choices, which of course you need to balance with your financial needs. And even if you have to go back to work you've outgrown, at least spend a little time planning for your next steps and invest in that. Maybe you take a course at night, or you join a group that's strong in the new function or industry that you want to pursue. Don't let financial pressure stop you from taking care of your career.

- Find new resources that are appropriate for where you are in your career. At a meeting of career counselors, I recently learned about Civic Ventures (www. civicventures.org), a nonprofit that helps baby boomers become a force for change in their communities. It offers a wide range of programs and resources for this population. If you're on the younger side of things, connect with your college, community resources, Peace Corps, Job Corps, City Year, and so on to find out what programs and guidance might help you find your next opportunity.

CHAPTER 33

FIND THE COURAGE
TO PITCH YOURSELF

Even if you're in sales and are good at pitching products or services, you might discover that it's an entirely different challenge to pitch yourself. Why is this so difficult for most of us?

I'll take you on a quick detour as a way of answering. When I worked as a corporate trainer and taught business writing, I used to tell my corporate students to be careful of the two Bs: begging and bragging. It's not effective to grovel to potential customers or to boast and toot one's own horn. Many people affected by job loss suddenly come face to face with these uncomfortable bookends: begging and bragging. So to set the record straight, you're not going to do either.

The worst way to motivate others to help you is to sound desperate and tell them you've got to have a job right now. And almost as destructive would be to brag and make it clear that you're the only one in the world with this particular gift, so you're obviously owed a job, and a good-paying one at that. Okay, so those extremes are out of the way, but it still feels weird to tell others what you're really good at or to provide examples of your accomplishments. Here's my theory as to why this feels so strange.

When we're working, we focus on what needs to get done. In my case, I have clients to see and need to know what their programs are as well as to review what we've already covered. I check my e-mail to make sure I haven't missed the latest version of their documents and review my notes from our previous meetings. I think about next steps for them before they come in so that I have a tentative plan in mind. And I make sure I've connected them to all the resources we have to offer. So what I'm not thinking about in the course of my work is me. I'm not saying to myself, "Oh, look at Jean. Isn't she clever? See how she helped this client get unstuck?"

But when thrown into looking for a new job, I have to do this. I have to turn the microscope from my clients onto myself. I have to figure out what makes me good at my job and come up with concrete examples that prove it. And I have to get over the discomfort and at the very least get less uncomfortable with talking about myself. This doesn't mean that I've now become a raging, egotistical maniac. Not at all. It simply means that I've done my homework and so can, in the course of a conversation (it could be an interview or a casual networking meeting), give others a good sense of who I am and what I'm good at.

One of the tools that I find useful in learning how to achieve this important relationship between self-promotion and listening is the target letter or e-mail (see appendix B). It's effective because it achieves just the right balance between what the reader needs and the writer's agenda. And by using bullets, it avoids the "I, I, I" problem that I see in a lot of clients' writing. Whether in writing or your spoken communications, you're focused on two major issues: What does the reader or listener need, what's on his mind, what's broken; and how can you help or what do you have to offer? In other words, you're talking about yourself, but not in a vacuum. Not in a monologue. Not by ignoring others. But ultimately it's really good to be able to articulate why that person or company should hire you.

As you put together your resume, practice saying out loud the accomplishments that are a major part of your professional experience. When you look at job postings or prepare for interviews and create the interview map we looked at in chapter 31, tell those stories to your search buddy or to someone you meet at a professional association meeting. Listen to yourself giving these examples. I promise you it will become less uncomfortable. Really good interviewing depends on high-quality listening, so if you're a quiet person and find this particularly challenging, take small steps and remember that your listening skills are going to help you. Who comes home from work and complains that too many people have listened to them?

PANIC IS NOT YOUR FRIEND

Penny had overcome tough obstacles in her life, and so she viewed job search as just another challenge. She had gone through a serious childhood illness as well as proving herself as both a woman and a minority (she was of Asian descent) in white-male-dominated financial services. She didn't let talk of a glass ceiling stop her and had worked her way up to a senior VP level. She was confident that her network was in place and that the right doors would open. And lastly, she was extremely articulate and very good at describing her accomplishments. If you're like me, you're thinking, this is going to be a piece of cake.

But it wasn't. The first sign of trouble was that Penny was easily distracted. Her husband worked at home, and when I asked about her activities during the day, it seemed as if his agenda eclipsed hers. I suggested she come to our office to work but she said she didn't need to do that. The second indication of trouble was her intense dislike of the job search process. To put it bluntly, she didn't want to do it, felt it was beneath her, and perhaps in some unconscious way thought she was owed a job (and a very good one, at that). This message didn't motivate her network, so although she had good relationships with people at a very senior level, her leads always seemed to peter out.

(continued)

(continued)

And lastly, panic set in. She had to have a job at least as senior as her last one (both in terms of scope and compensation), and she had to have it now. As I thought about ways to help her, I wondered whether there were steps she could take to build the muscles, skills, and tolerance she needed to succeed in this very important task. I suggested she organize her networking contacts in an Excel spreadsheet, I talked about the value of attending professional association meetings, I gave her examples of how other senior clients had created their search maps and daily schedules and how those had helped, and I invited her to join our senior team so that she could experience what other executives were doing. She was willing to join the team, but she politely turned down all my other suggestions. Her consistent message to me was, "I don't have time. I need a job now."

The sad irony of this attitude was that months went by and she was no closer to a job than she had been on day one. When clients ask me how long their search will take, one of the factors I always mention is tolerance of the process. If, like Penny, you're allergic to it and that gets in your way, it's probably going to take longer. If, like others whose examples you've encountered in this book, you're creative and willing to jump in with both feet, you're much more likely to land a new position quickly.

Quick Do's and Don'ts

Do:

1. Recognize that you're not going to beg or brag but build your skills so that you become more comfortable talking about yourself.

2. Take small steps. Tell the dog how you made a significant change at work, then try it out on a friend, and then work your way up to strangers.

3. Try anything that improves your overall communication skills. It could be joining a professional association, serving on a board, or tutoring a child. The most critical element is that you must be talking with other people.

Don't:

1. Confuse telling your clear accomplishment stories with being obnoxious. Job search is a classic give-and-take endeavor, so you're going to be listening and responding, not giving speeches.

2. Jump into networking and interviewing without a solid foundation. You need to be able to explain why you're looking for a new opportunity, talk about what you're good at (backed up by specific examples), and list some companies that are of interest to you (not based on job postings).

3. Let anger, disappointment, or any other negative emotions affect your communications. This is particularly important as you talk about your former company or how things are going in your job search campaign. (This is why it's not a good idea to start networking the day you are let go.)

Resources and Ideas

- Find a few people (ones you know or people you can listen to on the news) and analyze what makes them good communicators. Pay attention to their body language and how they use their voices, in addition to what they're saying.

- View learning a new and critical skill—pitching yourself—as an adventure. You might not have had to do this at your former company because people knew you and your work spoke for itself. But now that you're in the job market, it's essential and it will also make you more visible and successful at your next job.

- Realize that you're going to do this in your own way. When I take video of my clients in mock interviews, they often say (and I don't take this the wrong way), "But I don't want to sound like you!" That is just fine as long as your communications are effective. By reviewing the video together, we almost always agree on what's working and what might need some improvement. These subtle changes (more volume, effective gestures, solid eye contact, and so on) make a huge difference.

- Set up a schedule you can implement. For example, you might talk first with former coworkers, then neighbors or family, and a bit later, when you feel more confident, strangers you meet at professional meetings.

- Invest in improving your overall communication skills. Anytime you can improve these critical skills, there is tremendous payoff, whether you're working or looking for work. Quite a few of my clients have joined Toastmasters or taken Dale Carnegie courses or have attended communications classes at a local community college or adult education forum. They have found that their improved communications gave them an edge in both networking and interviewing.

- Reward yourself. I'm a great believer in doing something difficult and then recognizing that I did it and giving myself a reward. This can be small things—a cup of coffee with a friend, or buying a book, or something more special like planning a trip. (As my dog trainer constantly asks me during agility work when I forget to give my dog a treat, "Do *you* work for free?")

CHAPTER 34

THE ROLE OF LUCK, OR HOW ONE THING LEADS TO ANOTHER

Throughout this book, in many of the stories you've encountered so far, you've seen the outside activities job seekers have used as an important way to keep themselves motivated and refreshed. For some, training or a new certification is the answer. For others, volunteering, spending more time with family, mentoring, or coaching a sport is helpful. And you've also seen, in the example in chapter 21, how a simple bike ride led to a job offer, or how a job seeker in chapter 4 was helped by his daughter.

In this chapter, we're exploring how surprising things happen. I believe if you know about the diverse ways job seekers have been successful, you'll be better prepared to take advantage of what some would call luck. And by "luck," I mostly mean being at the right place at the right time. (And this rarely falls into your lap without a lot of hard work.)

In my first few years as a career counselor, I would never admit that luck mattered. I was learning from my clients, as well as from the firm that I worked for, both how to coach clients and what techniques were successful. Once in a while a client would say to me, "Boy, that was lucky," and I'd nod but not really admit that luck was part of the equation. But now, with 16 years under my belt, I see things a bit differently. What's most important to note here is that I'm not talking about gambling. This isn't a roll-of-the-dice kind of luck, but rather approaching a company at exactly the moment when they're thinking about a new role, new product, or new market and when they also have the budget to implement this idea.

As I've mentioned before, the bull's-eye of your search efforts is to get to decision makers—the ones who have the authority to hire you. And what's really difficult for many job seekers to understand is that you want to do this whether or not there is a posting. In other words, you're not letting what's posted on the Internet, or the positions handled by recruiters, determine your direction. You are proactively saying, "This is an interesting company that meets my criteria" (including industry, size, location, and anything else that's important to you). And then you're finding a way inside—through your network, through LinkedIn, your college alumni association or Career Development Office, or professional associations (and make sure to take advantage of the goldmine of directories), or by targeting the company directly (see appendix B).

But how do you know whether a company needs someone with your particular expertise? You don't, but you don't let that stop you. So one of the critical tasks you have to master is educating your network so that they understand what you're doing and why, and will then help you reach your goals and take advantage of luck. Here's a sample script:

> *Hi Bob. As you've probably heard, I'm no longer with XYZ corporation and am excited to be looking for a new position in Quality Assurance.*

You give Bob a moment to respond, and then say something like this:

> *I'm exploring large pharmaceutical companies in Central Jersey as well as emerging biotech firms in the Boston area, and I've put together a list of some of these. Could I send it to you to see what you know about any of these companies?*

Notice that I said "what" not "who." You want to take small steps—the best way to avoid rejection. And yes, you do want contacts, but those will come later.

Bob says okay but then tells you that he doesn't think any of them are hiring. This is where you have to help him understand what you're doing and why.

> *That's okay [even though it really isn't]. My goal is to get to the decision makers in these firms because that will help me understand their needs better. Then I can see where I might be a good fit.*

In other words, you're demonstrating here that you're in learning mode. You're exploring. You're open. And also, you're not desperate. This conversation—when you get in front of one of the hiring managers—is focused on the industry and how your particular background might be of help. It's not a "hire me because I need a job" message.

Bob tells you that you can e-mail the list to him and then you don't hear from him for a week. Because you have a networking spreadsheet that you check every day, you don't let this slip and politely remind him that you'd like his thoughts on your list of companies. Most times that does the trick. If it doesn't, switch methods of communication, so if you've been e-mailing, call, or vice versa.

FROM PROGRAMMING TO COOKING

Susan worked as a programmer and loved her job. She saw the value of her work, had a good relationship with her boss, enjoyed her coworkers, and stayed current with technology. After 18 years she was let go at the age of 53. She didn't seem bitter or angry, but expressed sadness at this very real loss. As we began to focus on her goals, she told me that she didn't know what she wanted to do, but couldn't see herself going back into programming. Somehow that chapter of her life was over, but she wanted to keep working and still needed income.

She spent some time talking with her friends and family about next steps, and she took several of our courses. After about a month, she signed up for a culinary course in a nearby city. Her whole demeanor changed from cautiousness to excitement. Every time we met my first question to her was, "What have you been making?" and then I'd hear about the proper way to hold a knife, how to slice potatoes, and the latest dish the class had created.

Susan really enjoyed her culinary training but wasn't sure how this was going to lead to a job or how she'd convince people that she no longer wanted to work as a programmer. She understood that she was not going to match her previous salary, but had adjusted her lifestyle and expenses and was fine with that. As we talked about ways she could use her new skills and interests, she thought she might be able to find a position as a helper in a commercial kitchen. Together we made a list of restaurants in the area, but this didn't work because they weren't interested in hiring someone with no restaurant experience.

As we continued to brainstorm, discussing both her contacts and the types of organizations that might hire her, she remembered that a friend of a friend owned a bed & breakfast. She called her friend, who gave her the contact information for the B&B owner. Susan decided that she'd send an e-mail first and then follow up with a phone call.

She used a variation of the target e-mail format, making it clear how excited she was to be in this new field and that she was open to any role. By the time we met again, she had a start date for her first job in culinary arts. So was this luck? Yes and no. It was lucky that she had a friend who knew someone and that this B&B owner had a need that Susan could fill. But Susan went about this the right way and even included in her e-mail to the owner how her past experience as a programmer gave her great attention to detail as well as the ability to follow complex instructions. So while she was new to cooking as a job, she brought with her important transferable skills. Rather than just work that brought in a paycheck, Susan now had a new career that was a good fit for her abilities and interests. Although she wouldn't have left her former position, she realized that this involuntary separation had given her the opportunity to make a radical career change.

Quick Do's and Don'ts

Do:

1. Prepare for luck. Make it easy for it to find you. By this I mean make sure that you have a clear, positive message about your goals and reach out to a diverse network.

2. Be open to suggestions that might sound a bit strange at first. Try to see yourself as someone on a journey that has many potential directions so that you're open to others' suggestions. Even if some of these ideas don't pan out, the more people who understand your message, the better.

3. Educate your network so that they're not closing the door because a company "has no postings."

Don't:

1. Close down conversations with negative statements such as "That won't work" or "They'll never hire me."

2. Assume your search will follow a logical and straight line. It can happen, but many times the path is more zigs and zags.

3. Let a negative response to your networking attempts stop you. Some people will be helpful; others won't. This is too important an endeavor to let a few wet blankets stop you. With a little help, some contacts who haven't been helpful may become so.

4. Waste people's time. Your job is to be well prepared and to know exactly what you want from each interaction while also remaining open to new ideas.

Resources and Ideas

It's fine to think about luck, but what should you do if you're stuck? How can you get yourself to try some of the networking suggestions covered earlier in this chapter, whether you're changing careers or looking for a position similar to your last one?

- Talk to others who are going through this process and ask them what they're doing and what seems to be working.

- Keep a journal so that you have evidence of your progress, even if it's subtle.

- Take a class on networking or interviewing or read a book on these topics so that you have some fresh ideas to try.

- Find your own way. I half-jokingly tell some of my clients that I'm bossy (which is true), but that I also recognize that this is their search and that they'll conduct it in a way that makes sense to them.

- Track what's working and what's not. There are lots of statistics about how jobs are found (with about 75 percent attributed to networking), but pay attention to your own data—what's giving you traction? What's making people want to meet with you?

- Maximize your chances of being lucky by being highly visible and by running a smart search. A client on my team just landed a wonderful job by contacting the recruiter who had placed him in his original job 25 years earlier.

- Be generous. This is a wonderful motivator and you'll find your network expanding if you're consistently forwarding job leads and industry information to others.

CHAPTER 35

SURVIVE THE INTERVIEW PROCESS

There are many fine books on interviewing, from ones that give you commonly asked questions to others that provide specific methodologies. As we look at the way forward, how you're making progress after the shock of job loss, and how to avoid common misconceptions about the process, I thought it would be helpful to share with you some general guidelines for interviewing, plus a dramatic example of "When everything goes wrong." This way, if you have a difficult interview or leave shaking your head wondering what on earth just happened, you'll know you're not alone.

Let's look first at some of the things you must do as you enter the interview process. First of all, it's critical that you be well prepared. This includes being comfortable (or less uncomfortable) with why you're looking for a new position, explaining who you are (this means your function and level), and having a good list of accomplishment examples so that you can prove you're good at your work, whatever it is. (A quick tip on this last one: Because it's often a bit strange to say how wonderful you are, you can put this in someone else's words: "My most recent boss liked to call me the *go-to person* because I'm good at solving problems.")

Second, you must research the company. A recruiter once told me that she was floored that job seekers would come to an interview with her and then ask, "What does the company do?" You want to know what the company does, how they're doing, and what's been in the news about them, and add these pieces of information to the interview map that we discussed in chapter 31. You also want to know about the people who will be interviewing you. So whether you're dealing directly with a company and HR (human resources) is setting up the interview, or if you're working with an outside recruiter, always ask for the list of people you'll be seeing, including names and titles. This allows you to tailor your map for each one and to practice difficult-to-pronounce names. It also helps reduce nervousness because you more or less know the interview schedule. (Just keep in mind that this often changes.)

Use your LinkedIn contacts to see whether you know someone who knows the people who will be interviewing you. If you do, see whether you can set up a quick conversation—again, as part of your interview preparation. Last, google their names so that if they have personal Web sites, you'll find them and then discover that they raise orchids or coach baseball. You have to use this personal information carefully, but if the interview is going really well and you sense that this is an open and relaxed person, you might comment about one of these personal interests. You never want anyone to be offended or nervous about the information you have.

About 10 years ago I had a client who was an HR director in the financial services industry. After 12 years with her company, Christine was let go. She decided that one of her goals was to explore new industries. She didn't dislike financial services, but she wanted to try something else. She attended a networking event in New York City and met a recruiter who was very interested in her background. Before long, the recruiter asked whether she could submit Christine for a senior-level position with a major pharmaceutical firm. Christine said fine and then asked me about it. My experience had been that the pharmaceutical industry likes to hire candidates who have already worked in its industry.

Christine had an asset that surprised me: She was a strong researcher and combined that strength in finding information with a broad and diverse network. So before she was called in for an interview, here's what she knew about the woman who would be her boss if she got the job: how long she'd been with the company, where she'd worked before, articles that she'd published, what professional groups she belonged to, and most surprisingly of all, why she hadn't been promoted from her current position.

When Christine told me about this, my advice was to be really careful because she almost knew too much. She agreed and used this information to be very well prepared, but of course didn't let on that she knew about the promotion issue. She and I practiced the "Why should I hire you when you haven't worked in this industry?" question and made sure that her accomplishments highlighted the ways she had succeeded with challenges in the past.

Christine got the job—a director-level job in a brand-new industry. And she did it through the help of the recruiter and her excellent preparation. And of course she was a fit; her skill set was what the company needed and she was able to convince them during the interview process that she would succeed in this role. Now let's look at a very different example, in which the interview process broke down (see the sidebar).

WHEN EVERYTHING GOES WRONG

Before I tell you Chris's story, I have to tell you that he didn't initially remember it but that it stuck in my mind because it was truly horrific. When I called him to ask permission to use this example, he burst out laughing, said yes, and then gave me the details.

Chris was a senior benefits manager. After several months of working really hard on his job search, he ended up with two interviews in one day in New York City. The first was for a university and the second for a bank. He made sure to leave plenty of time between the two interviews, and tried to get one of them rescheduled for another day, but couldn't. The university had told him that this was a simple screening interview that should take less than an hour and that they'd save the in-depth process for their shortlist.

Chris showed up 15 minutes early at the university and waited for the HR recruiter to come get him. He was shown into a conference room and the dean of the department came in to talk with him. This was supposed to last 15 minutes, but took almost 45. Other members of the search committee came in, sometimes together, other times individually, and the interview continued. The one hour turned into two and Chris began to worry. If he didn't finish in the next half-hour, he was going to be late for his bank interview, which was 40 blocks away.

He did his best to focus on the questions, and finally, when he had only 15 minutes before his next interview, they thanked him and he ran off the campus and hailed a cab. He was hyperventilating, looking at his watch, but thought he could make it. Just to be safe, he called the HR representative who had set up the bank interview and explained that he was stuck in traffic but should be there shortly. By the time he dashed in the building, he was 10 minutes late and didn't dare take time to go to the men's room. He told the receptionist who he was there to see and she looked at her directory and said that she didn't know of a person at the company with that name. Chris looked at his cell phone, now in a full sweat and found the phone number that he had just called. He gave that to the receptionist and was told to wait. He tried to sit down but couldn't because he was so jittery.

A young woman (Chris thought that she looked younger than his teenage daughter) finally came to get him. She didn't shake his hand and mumbled something he couldn't understand. He got into the elevator with her and they went up to the office. She put him in a small conference room and told him to wait. Ten minutes later she came back in but didn't sit down.

"Hiring manager isn't here," she said.

Chris didn't know what to say, but explained which job he was interviewing for.

The young woman, who never gave Chris her name, said that she was not from this office but had come in for the Christmas party. Chris nodded and smiled, trying to put her at ease, but wondered what to do next. It turned out she knew nothing about benefits, so she took the company handbook, sat down, and started asking him questions based on the information in the benefits section. He wondered whether things could get worse. They did.

Fifteen minutes into this agonizing process, the fire alarm went off. They were on the 23rd floor and another employee rapped on the door and told them to head down the stairs to the lobby. Chris grabbed his portfolio and coat, and followed the young woman and the other employees down the hall to the stairway. It was dim and crowded. As Chris took his first step down, his new leather shoes (which he had bought for the interviews), slipped and he fell, knocking over several other people as he bumped down the stairs on his rear end to the next landing.

He was stunned and hurt, but luckily nothing was broken. The woman didn't ask how him how he was or say anything. That was when Chris decided that the

(continued)

(continued)

interview was over. He limped down the rest of the stairs to the lobby, somehow managed to thank the woman for her time, left the building, and called his wife to tell her that he was coming home. It was the worst day of his entire search.

To give you the end of the story: Chris received several offers and accepted the position at the university. But on his first day on the job, his boss told him that he himself had taken an offer with a museum and wouldn't be working at the university. This left Chris with no one to report to. After three months, the university eliminated Chris's position. That was when Chris decided to go into consulting, and he has been successfully working in that capacity ever since. A last twist: Just a month ago he got a call from a recruiter who told him of a senior-level benefits opening at a museum in New York. When Chris guessed the correct museum (which is where his boss from the university had gone), he politely declined interviewing for it. He couldn't trust someone who had hired him knowing that his chances of surviving at the university were slim at best. And he had grown comfortable with consulting and his opportunities were expanding.

Quick Do's and Don'ts

Do:

1. Prepare well for interviews and do your best to expect the unexpected. This can include changes to the job itself, shifts in work location, and unprepared interviewers.

2. Stay light on your feet and don't let the feelings you have at the moment cause you to make a decision when you're upset and haven't had time to think through the pros and cons carefully. A difficult interview could lead to a good job.

3. Research both the company and the people you'll be seeing. The more you know, the better both your answers and questions will be. And remember, this is a two-way street: You're also interviewing them to see whether this is a place you'd like to work.

4. Don't assume you know what the interviewer or interviewers are thinking. I've had many clients think that things went terribly, only to find out a few weeks later that they're the top candidate.

Don't:

1. Wing it. This is never a good idea as interviews are too important and too difficult to get.

2. Jump to conclusions. When Chris interviewed at the bank, he never found out why the hiring manager wasn't there to see him. This didn't necessarily mean disinterest, but certainly showed they had some scheduling problems.

3. Expect clockwork. Interviews have to be fit in around people's busy schedules, and often things go wrong. You might have to come back another time so that you get to see everyone. In some cases, the whole interview might be cancelled.

4. Assume that the interview is an accurate picture of what it will be like to work at the company. I've had clients who have experienced wonderful interviewers and then disliked working for the company, and vice versa. Pay attention to what you experience, but keep an open mind.

Resources and Ideas

It's a good idea to talk to others about their interviewing experience so that you get a sense of what they've gone through. You might uncover trends, such as many companies using behavioral-based questions—the "tell me about a time when you…" type in which the interviewer wants details and to see you in action and find out how you solved problems, dealt with obstacles, and so on. And if you talk to enough people about this, you might come across some of the problems that happen during interviews: lack of company preparation, rude behavior, little consideration for the person being interviewed—no breaks, no time to eat, and more.

- Read a few books on interviewing. JIST Publishing has several excellent books on interviewing including *Interview Magic* by Susan Britton Whitcomb, *Next-Day Job Interview* by Mike Farr and Dick Gaither, and *The Career Coward's Guide to Interviewing* by Katy Piotrowski. Many books give you commonly asked sample questions. Practice answering some of these with your search buddy or a friend. (A really brave client of mine had his children pick the questions and then grill him.)

- Try to arrange networking meetings with people you don't know (but who could be helpful). This is great practice for interviewing. It's pressure, but not the intense pressure of an interview.

- Record yourself—with a webcam so that you can see and hear how you come across. But don't do this the day before an interview: It will only make you more nervous and you won't have time to adjust or fix any bad habits, such as saying "um" all the time or looking up at the ceiling every time you're asked a difficult question.

- Some career coaches suggest looking in the mirror as you practice for interviews. I've never been a fan of this method because I think it puts the focus too strongly on you and can make you feel more self-conscious.

- Prepare physically for interviews. This could include yoga or stretching for relaxation, eating a good breakfast or lunch before the interview so that you're energized, or taking a walk or working out to burn off some nervous energy.

Then give yourself plenty of time to get dressed and get to the interview so that you're not adding any more stressors to a stressful situation.

- Review your map just before you enter the building so that you remind yourself of what the company is looking for and how you match its requirements.

KNOW YOUR COMPETITIVE
ADVANTAGE

If a close friend or colleague asked you to help him describe himself and what he's really good at, you probably would find it fairly easy. And you might say things like, "You're really good with people," "You take technical information and make it easy to understand," or "You never miss an important detail or deadline." So why is this so hard to do for ourselves? My theory is that we have some twisted idea that we're not supposed to articulate our strengths, and as you saw in chapter 33, many of us worry about bragging.

One of the great pleasures of my work with clients is to watch the transformation that often happens during my time with them. To see the change from feeling hurt, confused, and angry to the first tentative steps in a new direction, and then to witness the confidence as this person starts networking and interviewing—successfully articulating how they've made a difference—never gets old. And as I mentioned at the beginning of this book, this is particularly exciting because I know that once you have these abilities, you have them for the rest of your career.

So how do you do this for yourself? There are many resources to help you, but let me give you a simplified list drawn from what I've seen work with my clients. First of all, this is not something you want to do at the beginning of your search unless you've been through this process before and don't feel devastated by job loss. But as you start to feel a bit less numb and confused, start making a list of the things you're good at. Put a little checkmark by the ones you like and read the list several times a day, adding to it or subtracting if you want. Look at your past performance appraisals and see whether there is language you can borrow for your list. As you get familiar with the job boards and read online postings, see again whether you can borrow some of that wording for your list. If a company wants someone who "works well independently and as part of a team," and that's true for you, write it down.

So let's say that after a week or two you have a pretty robust list. Now what should you do? Own it and believe it and be able to share it with others. This is the creepy part that can make you feel as if you have red ants crawling all over your skin. But my advice is do it, do it again, and don't let the awkwardness stop you. It's way too important. What you'll discover is that after a while, it's not so bad.

Let me share with you another of my favorite interview techniques. I think this will help you articulate what you're good at in a natural and effective way. It's called "ZAP" and stands for

- **Z**ero in on a problem or need.
- **A**sk questions.
- **P**rovide a short, positive answer with a selling point.

As discussed earlier, in both networking and interviewing, you're trying to have conversations. This is a natural way for people to share information. You ask me a question, I answer, but then I might ask you a question. It's back and forth, fluid, and if you eavesdrop in restaurants or on the bus, you'll hear examples of this all the time.

So let's say you're trying to get help to see whether you can use your manufacturing background in medical devices in another industry such as consumer products. And some very nice friend of a friend agrees to meet with you over coffee to talk about this because he's in consumer products. You bring your search map to the meeting, but first you need to talk. The conversation might go like this:

> *Thanks, Jim, for taking time to meet with me. Anne said you have an extensive background in consumer products, and as I look for a new opportunity in operations, I'm trying to figure out whether I can use my strong medical device experience in other industries.*

Now it's Jim's turn to talk. He says several things about consumer products and what the industry needs. But for him to really help you, he has to know more about you besides your industry challenge.

> *I'm particularly good at working with both union and nonunion shops. In my most recent position, I... (this is where you tell a really strong accomplishment story that illustrates your competitive edge).*

Again, you wait to see how Jim reacts. After asking a question or two (and of course keeping track of the time because you can't go over the agreed-upon time unless he says it's okay), you ask for help. This might be asking whether he'll take a look at the list of companies you're exploring, it could mean seeing whether he knows someone at your top pick, or you might ask about recruiters or professional associations. You're zapping or asking questions to get to the information that is going to help you. And as long as you balance that with careful listening, this should be a win-win situation. Jim should feel good at the end of your conversation, as should you.

So we've brought together two things here: probing and pitching. This is so much better than a script because it's natural and achieves the right balance between people. I'm sure you know people who aren't careful with this balance, and it's easy to feel beat up after a "conversation" with them. You've got an agenda, and a critical one at that: finding your next job. But genuine interest in others, although it might feel like a detour, is never a waste of time. As you build your muscles and learn how to articulate your edge or competitive advantage, remember "probe and pitch." This technique will help you when you start your new job, too.

PROBE AND PITCH

Here are two examples that illustrate how much can go into getting ready for interviews and the effectiveness of using probe and pitch to highlight your competitive advantage.

George had his Ph.D. and was what I would call a lifelong learner. He was an engineer and a Six Sigma Black Belt and had many other credentials. What I sensed from my first meeting with him was that he loved to learn. George was like a sponge and quickly read the manual we give our clients, took many of our classes, and came to his meetings with me upbeat and well prepared.

It took several months before he finally got an interview. His preparation for it was inspiring. He had a binder with charts and graphs that proved he understood what this company did and what they needed. He had copies of recommendations and awards, plus his certifications and his 90-day plan to address this company's engineering needs. I didn't see this binder until after his interview. When he showed it to me, I was very impressed. I had never seen something quite this extensive.

"So," I had asked him, "how did it go?"

"Not sure. They were hard to read."

"But did they react to your 90-day plan or other materials?"

"They looked at them but didn't say much."

I wondered if this was overkill. Did he go too far and somehow scare them? Could they be thinking, "If we hire this guy, is he going to make the rest of us look bad?"

Like everyone else, George had to wait for an answer. But after a few weeks, they told him that they didn't think he was a match. George became angry and resentful—angry they didn't get it and resentful of all his preparation. He understood that neither of us knew why the company made this decision, but I suggested that perhaps next time, he not reveal his materials all at once. This was just a hunch on my part, but I was thinking that when they knew him better, his impressive charts and plans might be less threatening. And like all interviewees, he had to be aware of the delicate balance between effective listening and presenting himself.

A second example highlights the importance of preparation in illustrating your edge. Grace really liked the interview map I showed you in chapter 31. She had an upcoming interview with a biotech company and wanted to knock them off their feet. Like George, she did extensive research on the company and the people she was going to see, and spent hours preparing for this all-day marathon. (She was going to be interviewed by seven people.) Grace took the map preparation a step

(continued)

(continued)

further: She created a folder for each of the seven interviewers and in it included a copy of her map, her business card, copies of her top awards, and of course her resume. On the outside of each folder, she printed the interviewer's name and title as well as the company name.

Grace was pumped—she was so excited to finally have an interview and she gave it 150 percent of her energy. When it was over she told me that she could barely drive home. The next day she sent seven individualized thank-you e-mails. A few days later, she called me.

"Jean, I haven't heard anything."

"What did they say about their timing?" I asked.

"I don't know. That I'll hear in a week, or two."

"Okay, so it hasn't been a week, has it?"

"No, but I think this is really rude."

From here we discussed the time warp that many job seekers experience—how time when you're working goes by quickly, but when you're in transition it can feel as if it's barely moving. So a day or a week could easily feel like forever to Grace—especially because she was a high-energy, fast-paced person. By the following week she was furious and told me that if they called her now she would give them a piece of her mind and tell them that this was a terrible way to treat people. I begged her to call me first and not to say anything without careful thought. I explained that she had to separate her feelings about the interview process from an objective look at this opportunity if she got an offer.

After three weeks, she couldn't stand it any longer, e-mailed the HR person, and found out that they'd hired another candidate. As her anger spiked again, I tried to help her understand that she had done a really good job, but that she couldn't control what the company had decided. That was out of her hands. And I complimented her on her thorough preparation, which I knew had made it more difficult for her to wait and then be turned down. Grace was so upset that she had to stop searching for almost a week.

I would never say don't do what George and Grace did. I would simply caution you that as you prepare for interviews and learn how to share your competitive advantage, keep your expectations in check. Don't confuse your standards with a company's. Don't assume that there are universal courtesy rules that they'll follow. Prepare and prepare well, share your knowledge in subtle ways, probe and pitch, give yourself time to recover from the extreme effort of interviewing, and then invest in something else. I don't think I've ever seen a client get an offer from every interview she went on, so balance your effort with ways to protect yourself. And remember, if you're interviewing, you're getting really close to the finish line. And that is wonderful.

Quick Do's and Don'ts

Do:

1. Learn how to talk about yourself effectively. This means get familiar with your own background so that you can give specific examples of the ways you've made a difference. And do your best to articulate what you bring to the table that may be unique.

2. Prepare thoroughly for both networking and interviewing. Research the company as well as the people you'll be meeting, and create a list of questions.

3. Practice talking about yourself so that it becomes less uncomfortable, and remember to use pitch and probe.

4. Use tangible examples if you have them. Few things are more effective than show and tell. (This could be an object that you helped design, or possibly a certificate or award that you received.)

Don't:

1. Bore people with long, memorized, or overly rehearsed speeches.

2. Eclipse listening with your own agenda. As I was helping a new client prepare for an interview, I asked her whether she had received any feedback from her previous interviews. She said she had been told that she talked too much and didn't demonstrate interest in others. We worked on how to adjust her communications so that this wouldn't happen again. But when we wrapped up, she talked for 10 minutes without stopping, although she knew I had another appointment.

3. Assume that your preparation for an interview was a waste of time if the company doesn't hire you. These are two separate issues and you always want to be well prepared. This is never wasted effort.

Resources and Ideas

If you're stuck trying to figure out what your competitive advantage is, consider these ideas. And keep in mind: Your edge might be something small, such as keeping track of details, that you think doesn't matter. But as you test it with others, you'll come to see that it makes a difference.

- Come up with a list of questions or a short survey that you can use to get feedback from others on your competitive advantage. You might ask former coworkers, "How have I made a difference?" or "What do you think I'm really good at?" or "When you think about the work I've done, what stands out?"

- Develop your listening skills. A good listener will always do well in both networking and interviewing. You're a captive and motivated audience, so take advantage of that to impress people with your interest in them. And pay attention to nonverbal cues. Many times you can see when you're addressing an interviewer's needs by his or her posture and facial expressions.

- Be subtle about probing; but if you can, find out more about a company's or an individual's needs. This will ensure that your accomplishment stories hit the bull's-eye and illustrate your competitive advantage.

- Draft a copy of the target e-mail format in appendix B and practice reading it aloud. What is it that you're really good at? Even if you decide never to send this as an e-mail, it will help you describe and provide proof of your strengths. One client described her competitive advantage this way: "I'm the best number-two person you can find. I will work well behind the scenes to make sure that my boss has what he or she needs to succeed." This kind of statement shows great confidence and self-knowledge.

CHAPTER 37

MEASURE YOUR PROGRESS

As I've mentioned earlier, this is not an all-or-nothing game. Most likely you will see lots of small signs of progress and moving forward before you get to a job offer. But how do you know how you're doing? What are the footholds in this slippery process? And what are realistic goals you can set for yourself?

First of all, you must have a strong foundation for your search, which includes the following:

- An effective resume (more on how to road-test that in a minute)
- A list of three to five references (one to two should be a boss or boss's boss)
- Clear verbal communications about why you were let go (unless you're a recent college graduate; and then you'd talk about your major and interests), what you're looking for, and your competitive advantage (see chapter 36)
- A networking spreadsheet so that you can see who's in your network, whether they have your resume and search map, and when you need to follow up
- A job search schedule so that you're accountable each day (see appendix A)
- A search map that outlines your goals and includes a list of companies (see appendix C)
- A business card (see appendix E)—helpful for networking
- An implementation timeline (see appendix G), which gives you a critical way to measure progress

Make sure you have these resources in order and that you're following your implementation timeline. This is not a rigid document, but it gives you a framework so that you know, for example, that by the end of the month your resume will be completed and the following week you'll have your references in place. If something happens and you can't stick to your timeline, revise it, but do your best to make up the time you lost. And if you consistently aren't meeting your goals, you probably need to revise your job search schedule and either add more hours to your search each day or change what you're doing.

Let's say you've got this foundation in order but you're worried about your resume. As one of my clients put it, "There's something wrong with my resume because my phone isn't ringing." Get feedback from other people in your field (these may be former coworkers). Join a professional association if there is one for your function (HR, IT, Operations, and so on) or industry (chemicals, manufacturing, cosmetics, food, and so on). Ask for help from recruiters, who see a lot of resumes and very often have excellent suggestions. If you're still unsure, read a book on resumes (these can be very specific such as a book on resumes for teachers) and compare the formats in the book with yours.

I like to think of a resume as a living document because it almost always changes. You go on an interview and someone asks you a really great question about how you solved a particular problem, and you realize later that you didn't mention this accomplishment in your resume. Or a recruiter tells you that it's too hard to see the new certifications you have. So don't be afraid to revisit your resume and to revise it.

What I think isn't helpful, however, is having too many cooks. You don't want to go around in circles because one person prefers a particular format or another thinks you need more adjectives. Even career professionals have different opinions, although most of us agree on the basics. So once your resume is "done," get it out into the market because that will give you productive feedback.

With your foundation in order, it's a good idea to take a few minutes at the end of every week to review what you've done and what has happened. Where is your resume posted? Are you getting any calls? Who have you reached out to in your network? Who do you need to nudge or revisit? Then jot down a few things that moved your search forward. These can be small steps or large: I ordered my business card, I completed my search map, I made a call that I really didn't want to make, two recruiters called me, and so on. And then write yourself a note so that on Monday morning you know what you're going to do. As you look at your search schedule, you want to make sure you don't forget to send your resume to the recruiter who called you yesterday or to follow up on the new leads you got from someone you met at a networking meeting.

When that little voice tells you, "But I don't have a job yet," take a deep breath, review your progress, adjust your strategy if there are clear signs that certain things aren't working, and you will get there. A senior client who just landed a terrific job a few weeks ago figured out that his search took him almost a year and that he had sent out more than 1,000 e-mails, had more than 300 job search conversations, went on 12 interviews in person (three times finishing in second place), had 35 phone interviews, built a consulting practice, and turned down 4 offers. His advice:

> *Don't let anyone tell you that your market value has decreased. Stick to your goals, get past the "Don't you have a job yet?" questions, and remember how important it is to have your life priorities in the right order. At the end of the day, it's just a job and it's good to have the money to pay the bills; but remember everything that surrounds you, especially those who have helped in this difficult time.*

This does *not* mean that your search will take this long, but in this case my client's goal was not to compromise on either the scope of the job or the compensation, so it took longer. And he had the finances and the motivation to sustain it.

SMALL STEPS, BIG RESULTS

Some of the clients I work with decide—either early in their search or later after they've been in the process for a while—to take a radically different direction and start their own businesses. Will's experience gives a perfect example of the many small changes he made that led to big results.

Will was a senior HR professional and loved his work. He dealt with a wide range of issues, from supporting the employees at his company to preparing performance evaluations, testing, managing compensation, and making sure company policies were in line with the organization's mission. Will had a strong network in place and had been through the job search process before, so he was confident that things would go well.

He got his materials in order and organized his networking contacts in a spreadsheet so that he could follow up effectively. He was active in several HR organizations and stayed up to date in his field. And he was good at balancing his efforts between the published job market (online postings and recruiters) and the unpublished one (leads found through networking and targeting). He had a few interviews and did well, but didn't get an offer. At about the three-month mark, I noticed that he looked a bit discouraged. When I asked him about this, he said he was fine and then asked me whether anyone was getting a job in this economy. We discussed this for a while, he made some adjustments to his search map (focusing more on small and midsized companies), and we agreed that we would monitor this together.

At our next meeting Will told me that he wanted to explore consulting and that he was thinking of setting up his own practice. We talked about the pros and cons of starting a business, and I connected Will to our entrepreneurial resources. This is where the small steps came in: Will methodically researched what he would need to do to launch his own firm, and day after day, he took action so that after only a few months, he had his first client. He did such a fine job with that work that the company signed him on for another contract. Will also found that if he applied for standard HR positions, he was sometimes able to pitch his business as a cost-effective solution for the company. Although he didn't get back to his former compensation in the time he was with me, he had a strong foundation and a growing business and was enjoying his new role as an independent consultant.

Quick Do's and Don'ts

Do:

1. Create a realistic search schedule (see appendix A) and implementation time-line (see appendix G). I can't tell you how many clients I've had who are stunned that they don't have an offer a few weeks after they've been let go.

2. Build a strong foundation and make sure you have all the materials in the list at the beginning of the chapter in good order.

3. Evaluate your progress each week and recognize that you are moving forward. Adjust your strategy if you get stuck.

4. Get help if you can't see the forest for the trees. It's often a lot easier for someone outside your search to see the progress you're making.

Don't:

1. Assume that nothing is happening just because your phone isn't ringing. There is almost always a lag between effort and response.

2. Keep banging your head on the same wall. One of the most discouraging searches I have ever been part of involved a person who would only use online ads and wouldn't do anything else despite clear evidence that this wasn't working.

3. Let discouragement stop you from following your plan. You've made a commitment to a process and have to keep going. (But short breaks and rewards are just fine.)

4. Fall into all-or-nothing thinking. This is a back-and-forth, up-and-down endeavor and it's critical that you recognize progress, especially the small steps.

Resources and Ideas

When you look back at how you got through other difficult times, you might discover that you reached out to others, joined groups, used research to give yourself options, and slowly made progress. When we're in crisis mode our world shrinks because we hunker down to do what we need to do to survive. But in job search, we need to expand so that we're enriched by others' ideas and connections. Here are some questions that may help you measure your progress:

- Is your network growing? (I get really nervous when clients tell me that they've exhausted their network, and I always think of both meanings for "exhausted.")

- Are people receptive to and motivated by your message?

- Are you getting referrals to others and promptly following up on them?

- Are you consistently thanking everyone who has helped you?
- Can you demonstrate that you're open to new ideas?
- Is your image (body language and grooming) supporting your value?
- Are you generous to others?
- Do you attend professional associations or other groups? (This is really important because it gets you out of the house and you never know who you might meet.)
- Are you well prepared for networking meetings and interviews and respectful of others' time?

CHAPTER 38

WHEN ALL ELSE FAILS

Here's a tricky balance issue: You want to assume that your search will go well and that you'll have a new job in a reasonable period of time, but you also need to be prepared for a longer search. How can you do both of these things at once?

In your implementation timeline (see appendix G), it's a good idea to list obstacles you might encounter in your search and how you plan to deal with them. Let's say you don't have a college degree and all the ads you've seen require one. You clearly need a strategy for getting around this. Or perhaps your past salary was higher than what the market seems to be offering. What will you do? But in addition to thinking through these obstacles and your ideas for dealing with them, you also want to have a plan B in place so that if your search takes longer than expected, you have income.

As discussed earlier in the book, some people's plan Bs involve working in a new way, as Will did in chapter 37. He's still in HR, but is now a consultant instead of an employee. Others might choose a more radical change from their previous work, such as driving a limo or delivering newspapers (or in my case, working in a flower shop), but one that brings in some money and reconnects them with work.

So let's say you have a plan B in place, but you're not at the point where you need to implement it, and you feel stuck. Your efforts of looking for a job feel like drudgery. Day after day you make real efforts but you're worn out and discouraged. And you really don't believe that you'll ever work again. What should you do? If you look back at the suggestions at the end of chapter 1, you'll remember that some find help from therapy, others from physical exercise, and still others from volunteering. A new project or hobby can be another way to go. In my opinion, the real issue here is self-care—something most of us aren't very good at. So when recently working with a client who was stressed out after an intense round of interviews that didn't lead to an offer, here's what I asked her:

- What do you do for fun?
- What would feel like a break or mini-vacation?
- Why are you spending all day every day on the Internet? Can you break that habit?

- If you were advising a friend who was in your situation and your friend was worn down and tired, what would you tell him or her to do?

What I discovered from asking her these questions was that she loved to play baseball with her two young sons. I pushed a little and made her commit to baseball games over the weekend. I suggested she put a piece of paper with a large *X* on it over her computer monitor so that she wouldn't unconsciously log in and surf the Internet. And I made her come up with one other pleasurable activity, which in her case was baking. So she agreed to make bread over the weekend—something she hadn't done in years.

You might be thinking, "But how did those things get her closer to a new job?" And my answer is that they restored this person, gave her back parts of herself that were lost, and made her feel more confident. Job searching is hard work, so it must be sustained with good self-care. The obstacle that many people have to get over to do this is a false sense that this is wrong—that they're selfish if they care for themselves. And sure, if you take this to an extreme and only care for yourself, then there's a problem. But balancing the demands of finding a new job with smart ways of caring for yourself will make you more successful. In the sidebar, there's one of the wildest examples of this I've encountered in my 16 years as a career coach.

THINKING OUTSIDE THE BOX

Ted was highly educated—he had his Ph.D. in physics—and held a senior-level position with a German company that made sophisticated instruments. He loved his job but didn't show any signs of anger or loss as a result of being thrown into transition. He asked a lot of questions but was also generous with his knowledge. One of the things he taught me was the benefit of taking notes and reviewing them. To this day, that is one of the main ways I prepare for my meetings with my clients.

Things went along smoothly for the first four months, but as Ted interviewed and didn't receive any offers, he grew discouraged. So we discussed self-care and I asked him some of the questions in the preceding list. These didn't resonate with Ted, so I tried a different angle and said, "If you were going to think outside the box and do something you wouldn't ordinarily do, what would it be?" He asked if he could think about it and I said that would be fine.

We had a few more meetings and were focused on interview preparation. But then, because I had reviewed my notes before my meeting with him, I asked him what he had come up with that would be something different. He had a slight smile on his face and said to me, "Can't you see it?"

I looked at him carefully but couldn't see anything that looked different. He leaned closer and pulled his hair back from his forehead. Then I could see hundreds of tiny scabs on his scalp, but I still didn't get it. He saw the confused look on my face and burst out laughing.

(continued)

(continued)

"I got hair plugs," he said, "as you told me to do something outside the box."

I think I stopped breathing. "You what?"

"My hair was thinning and it bothered me, so I went to a specialist in the city, paid a lot of money, and I'm now waiting for my new hair to sprout."

I was still speechless.

Now Ted was concerned about me. "Don't worry, I did it because I wanted to do it. I just needed a little nudge."

"Wow," I told him, "you really shocked me. I never would have guessed."

I was thinking to myself that I was going to have to be more careful in what I say to my clients because this wasn't exactly what I had in mind. But Ted was fine with it. And in the next few weeks, his hair got a bit thicker and he was pleased with the results. He landed a good job about a month later. At our final meeting we had a good laugh about his hair. He teased me by saying that he was now convinced that he got his offer because he looked so good. We shook hands and I wished him the best. And to this day I have never told another client to think outside the box!

Quick Do's and Don'ts

Do:

1. Create contingency plans so that if your search goes on longer than expected, you know what you'll do.

2. Take care of yourself during this demanding process. Find the things that restore you so that this doesn't become drudgery.

3. Work hard on your search but don't let it eclipse your whole life. I can't tell you how many examples I've seen of positive results coming from short breaks and rewards.

4. Research opportunities for training, whether in your existing area of expertise or something new. Adding new skills will broaden your market and also give you an area where you can see immediate results.

5. Use volunteering as a way to expand your network. A neighbor I helped with her job search really liked this idea because she's shy and realized that it would be easier to connect with others when involved in a project.

Don't:

1. Become a job search machine. You'll wear yourself out and won't be presenting your best self to others.

2. Assume you know how and when you'll discover your next opportunity.

3. Get stuck. If one method isn't working, try another.

4. Tell your network that there are no jobs out there. This is a depressing message.

5. Be unwilling to compromise. Sometimes you might have to take a small step back to move forward.

Resources and Ideas

Because we've been talking about ways to care for yourself while looking for a new position, take a moment to think about what your outside activities say about you. Recently, several of my clients have been asked at interviews, "What have you been doing aside from looking for work?" Here are examples from clients I've been working with in the past year and what their activities say about them:

- Cheerleading coach: An interest in young people plus high energy because this is a demanding activity
- Red Cross board member: Well connected, concerned about the community, a great resource during disasters
- Optimist Club founder: Entrepreneurial, generous to others, interested in young people (that's a major part of this organization's mission)
- Op-ed writer: Excellent communication skills, connected to community, interested in politics
- Ballet dance instructor: Physically active, good with children, artistic
- Cook for the Ronald McDonald House: Works well with a team, concerned about children with critical illnesses, supportive
- Habitat for Humanity volunteer: Skilled with tools, concerned for those who need low-cost housing, physically active
- Soup kitchen server: Good with people from all walks of life, generous to others

CHAPTER 39

MOTIVATING OTHERS TO HELP YOU

As we near the end of this wild ride of going from job loss to career resilience, I want to focus on one of the major keys to success: motivating others to help you. This is critically important because loners have a much more difficult time finding work. As you saw in Bob Morgan's story at the end of part 2, he compares networking to "dental extraction." There are many negative ideas about what networking is that prevent job seekers from connecting effectively with others. And although networking and motivating others to help you aren't synonymous, there's a lot of overlap because the most successful networkers have mastered this critical skill.

So what can you do to make others want to help you? Let's look at this in list form and then in more detail:

- Be prepared.
- Be polite.
- Reciprocate (share information and resources).
- Be upbeat.
- Be curious and open (ask for advice).
- Take action.
- Follow up.
- Don't stop.

By now you know what you need to be prepared. You looked at a list in chapter 37. And I know it sounds silly to include manners or being polite, but these are the oil that greases the machine. They're important—especially as motivators. At the end of every week in my own search campaigns, I'd ask myself, "Who do I need to thank?" And then I'd send off notes so that those people felt appreciated and also to remind them that I was still out there looking.

When you read Ken Paul's story at the end of part 3, you'll see that he became an information-sharing expert. He was willing to go almost anywhere to meet with people, and he always offered to buy them coffee. The critical thing to keep in mind here is that you are not coming to these meetings empty handed, but instead have valuable information to share. This might include who's hiring, which professional associations are worth joining, salary trends, and interviewing practices, as well as specific information on the companies you're targeting.

When I explain to my clients how to call a company to get the name of a hiring manager, I like to say, "I use my Girl Scout voice." This means I'm upbeat. It's sounds strange, but if you're cheerful you'll get more information than if you sound discouraged. In networking meetings, you can be honest, but you must be very careful not to drag people down. So you might say something like, "My search has gone on a bit longer than I expected, and I came close to an offer with a few companies. So now I'm seeking outside advice so that I can fine-tune my efforts and make sure I'm conveying my ability to help a company with its (fill in your area of expertise)."

As I listen to clients on my team talk to each other, I keep an ear out for negativity because nothing shuts down networking more quickly. So if one person says, "Hey, Joe, have you thought about contract work?" And then Joe says, "I'm not interested. I want a permanent job," Joe has effectively told the other person that he is not going to listen and that, furthermore, his idea was a stupid one. End of conversation. If Joe really isn't interested in contract work but wants to keep the connection alive and active, he could say, "Thanks, that's a good idea. I've got to think about that more carefully because my initial goal was to look for permanent positions. Do you know some contract firms?" That's a radically different message, but it still doesn't commit Joe to contract work.

Why do we like people who are curious and open? Because their attitude is infectious and it's flattering to have someone ask us questions and show interest in our opinions. Remember this when you're interviewing—you want to show intense interest in the people you meet at the company. As you talk and ask questions, you'll find out what their challenges are, what needs improving, and what it's like to be an employee at this company.

Taking action after someone has given you advice or a lead is critical because it's one of the best motivators around. If I say to you that I think you'd really benefit from attending a meeting of the ASTD (American Society for Training and Development), and then you go to a meeting and tell me about it after, I'm motivated to come up with more ideas that might help you because you took action. If for some reason you can't take action, make sure to explain it. You might say, "Thanks, Jean. That's a great idea, but because I have an interview this week, I'm going to hold off and attend the following week. Is that okay?" Because you gave me your plan, I still feel that you're valuing my advice, and of course I understand that the interview needs to come first.

Follow-up, in my opinion, becomes one of the most important activities in a search once it's launched because it is through follow-up that we get to the best help. This is because our contacts get to see that we're professional, motivated, and sincere. We're treating our search for a new opportunity as a job—and an important one, at that. It's on the third or fourth contact, when you've proven yourself to the person you're networking with, that you're most likely to get the gold—the best connections or information.

One of the big worries here is being a pest. So what's the difference between good, professional follow-up and being a pest? Timing and how you do it. If, for example, I promise to get you a name at a company that's of interest to you, you need to give me a few days to get to it. But if, after three or four days you don't hear from me, politely either call me or e-mail me, but don't do both and don't then follow up again five minutes later. Give me time to get to it and then thank me when I do and take action so that I know you're using this connection.

And lastly, don't stop. You can't give up because finding another job is way too important. You can take short breaks; it's good to take care of yourself and have some fun (very few things get between me and my tennis drill on Friday afternoons). But you must keep at it—for yourself and your family, and to send a strong positive message to your network.

A ROCK CLIMBER TRIUMPHS

Violet was a petite, African American CFO who was very good at her job. As a child she had fallen in love with math; and to her, numbers were poetry. She had worked hard to make it to a senior level in finance and was devastated by her job loss. After months of searching and at least seven interviews, she asked me for advice because she couldn't figure out why she still didn't have an offer.

Violet and I had done extensive interview practice, so I was pretty sure her answers were strong and concise. She understood how to ask questions, and her body language supported her positive and upbeat message. We discussed this together, trying to figure out what she might do differently. When we had started our work together and were putting together her resume, she had listed rock climbing at the end of her resume under an Outside Interests heading. When I asked her why she wanted to include this, she told me that being a woman and being small, she didn't want people assuming she was weak or afraid of risks. And she was right— interviewers seemed to love to ask her about her rock-climbing experiences— where she went, her close calls, and so on.

Finally I asked her to tell me everything she did from the moment she entered the building for an interview. She shrugged her shoulders and asked me why that mattered. I told her that something wasn't working and that we needed to figure out what it was. And what I found out amazed me: Violet, in an effort to be assertive and show her strength, was not allowing the interviewer to tell her where to sit. She was simply walking into the room or office ahead of the interviewer and plunking herself down where she wanted to sit.

"Oh," I told her, "you need Etiquette 101."

"What are you talking about?" Violet asked.

"You need to let the interviewer run the show. You're the guest and he or she will tell you where to sit. It's fine to be strong and assertive, but you mustn't scare them."

Violet agreed to make this subtle but real change in her next interview, which was with a leading cosmetics company. And she got the job. Of course, I can't prove that this was a result of her change in etiquette, but I do believe it helped. So if you look back at the list of the ways to motivate others to help you, you'll see that Violet, by asking for help, gave me a chance to brainstorm with her. In other words, she was open and willing to learn. And I wouldn't be surprised if the company that hired her sensed that at the interview. It's an attractive quality, so even if it's a struggle for you, try to send this strong, positive message as you talk with others.

Quick Do's and Don'ts

Do:

1. Motivate others to help you. It's a critical part of the search process.

2. Experiment so that you discover the best motivators for your network.

3. Ask for feedback if something isn't working.

4. Make follow-up an important part of your daily activity. And if one method isn't working, try another.

Don't:

1. Keep your plans to yourself.

2. Forget courtesy. It's a fantastic motivator.

3. Assume that if you don't hear from someone, they're not interested. It's your job to follow up.

4. Be afraid to learn new skills to get you to your next job.

5. Equate networking with cold calling. It's not, and you aren't asking others to find you a job. You're simply enlisting their help as you run a professional and balanced search.

Resources and Ideas

When managers are being considered for promotion, they sometimes are put through what is called 360 feedback or a 360-degree review. This is basically a way to find out from others (this may include peers, subordinates, managers, outside vendors, and so on), through a controlled and anonymous process, how they're perceived. I'm not suggesting something this complicated for you. But you could do an informal survey of past coworkers and your direct reports (if you had them) to find out whether you need to do any fine-tuning, as Violet did, to be more effective in your job search. Here are questions you might ask:

- If you were going to describe my work to someone who didn't know me, what would you say?
- Can you come up with three or four adjectives that you think accurately describe me? (Examples would be generous, high energy, organized, thoughtful, attentive to detail, and so on)
- Is there anything you think I need to work on that would make my search more effective?
- Do you have any feedback on how I'm approaching people (networking)?
- What do you see as my greatest strengths?

These questions may feel a bit uncomfortable because the focus is on you and what others think of you. Of course, you need to be careful about who you select. It's probably not a good idea to ask for feedback from someone you haven't gotten along with well or others who don't know you well. The best people are ones who have seen you in action and who you think could provide helpful advice.

Lastly, don't keep score. That is not an effective way to network or get people to help you. I see this frequently with clients asking others for LinkedIn recommendations. The script goes something like, "I'll write a recommendation for you if you'll write one for me." That's not nearly as effective as an open and unencumbered offer to write a recommendation for someone whose work you know and believe in. And if they offer to write one for you, fine. If they don't, that's fine, too.

CHAPTER 40

A PERSONAL STORY: FROM VOLUNTEER TO NEW CAREER

As mentioned in the introduction, I fell into the outplacement field (career coaching) in the mid-1990s through an odd set of circumstances. I had worked as a corporate trainer, flying all around the country giving classes on business writing and presentation skills. Then I had transitioned back to writing and spent five years writing press releases, articles, and monographs for an educational company. That work ended and I was stuck because I really didn't want to go back into training and there didn't seem to be other writing assignments nearby. (It was at this time that I was also writing fiction and trying to get that published—a huge uphill battle.)

My son was 9 and my daughter was 19—just off to college. My husband was working at a local college as an adjunct, which meant not great pay and no benefits. So I was under real financial pressure to find work, but I knew more about what I didn't want to do than what I did. (What I tell my clients now when I hear a similar message is that this is a great place to start. Knowing what you don't want to do gives you the beginning of a plan.)

From watching the news, I had felt drawn to the coverage of the war in Bosnia. What struck me was a haunting thought: If it were me losing my home, having my children injured or killed, and experiencing the devastation of war, what would I want others to do? And the answer was clear: help. I would hope that someone somewhere would care enough to reach out to me—not because they knew me, but because they knew of the suffering that the people of a war-torn country were experiencing.

So that was the germ, the idea that began to have a life of its own. Through my church I found a local woman who was involved in refugee resettlement. I asked her to come talk to a group of us about what was involved in sponsoring a refugee family. I started gathering information and making lists. I spoke to our vestry and began thinking of ways to raise money. What became clear very early was that others (some in my church and some from the community at large) were also concerned and wanted to help. It was like kindling that needed a spark. I can't tell you why I couldn't just say to myself, "Well, it's a war and it's unfortunate, but I can't do anything about it." I felt driven to try. And with such wonderful support, the concept of sponsoring a refugee family began to feel like something we could make happen.

After a few months, we had the beginnings of a plan in place. But for some reason, the woman from the refugee resettlement group couldn't find us a family. We waited, we called and followed up, but nothing was happening. I started asking around and was connected to the Lutheran refugee resettlement program, which turned out to be better organized. They had a representative in the Department of Immigration and knew how to get to the United Nations High Commissioner for Refugees (UNHCR) to find families who had been given refugee status.

More weeks went by and I started collecting things a family would need. It was magical: I'd make an announcement in church that I wanted pots and pans, dishes, towels, and so on, and within a few days a large box would appear on my front porch. I discovered that I loved doing this and was good at convincing people that they could part with their extra belongings.

The committee had now grown to more than 20 people—the bulk from my Episcopal church in Yardley, St. Andrew's, as well as another nearby church, Incarnation. We wrote about our efforts and had articles published in the local paper, so we gathered more volunteers. We held fund-raisers and raised more than a thousand dollars. But we still didn't have a family.

In May 1994, I received a call from the Lutheran immigration people: "You have a family." I was stunned that it was going to finally happen and asked what they could tell me about them. I found out it was a family of five and that the youngest child was under 2 years old. The Lutherans didn't know what languages they spoke or when they would arrive. But they told me to be ready because I probably would have very little notice.

The rector of my church didn't live in the rectory, so I convinced her and the vestry that we could use that house for interim housing, especially because church school (which had classes in the building) was almost finished for the year. So now the committee moved into high gear and brought in beds, clothing, nonperishable food, toys, and toiletries so that when we got the call, we'd be ready. We had specialized tasks: One person would help them apply for public assistance (refugees are eligible for this), another would cover doctors' visits, yet another dental work (which turned out to be a huge job), several others transportation, tutoring for the children, registering them for school, and so on.

On the Wednesday before Memorial Day I was told that the family would be arriving on Friday night at the Philadelphia airport. I was given their names and the flight number and that's all. My minister, Charlene, found someone nearby who could make a sign that said "Welcome" in Bosnian and on Friday night Charlene and I stood at the gate in the airport with our sign. It was one of the most exciting moments of my life—not knowing what was ahead, not knowing who they were, but deep down believing that this was right and that it would all work out.

A tall man looked at us and our sign. Next to him was his wife, carrying a baby, and next to her the two girls, ages 8 and 9. They smiled and we smiled back. And then we did what comes most naturally—we hugged each other. Charlene, who spoke German, tried that out. No luck. I tried French. That didn't work either. So we pointed and said things that didn't make any sense to them, but we kept smiling so that they knew we were glad they made it. We all went to collect their luggage and then Charlene and I went to get the car. We told them to wait, hoping they knew we weren't deserting them. It was almost 11 p.m. by the time we got to the rectory. We helped them carry their bags inside, showed them the food in the kitchen, and pointed to them so that they knew it was for them. We went upstairs and showed them the bedrooms and bathroom.

I was suddenly terrified that there would be a fire or some other disaster and that they wouldn't know what to do. There was a 911 sign above the phone, but I realized they couldn't call because they didn't speak English and didn't know their address. Using gestures (and sign language, because I had been working with the deaf and couldn't stop myself), I tried to explain that I would be back in the morning. I showed them how to lock the front door. And we said goodnight.

Charlene and I hugged each other and that was the end of the first day—their first day in America. When I tell my clients that looking for work is rarely a straight line, I think of this experience and how it helped me. For one thing, it gave me something to do that made me feel useful. It also connected me to people—my committee and the Bosnian family. And it became a magnet; before we knew it, we had an interpreter, a retired ESL teacher for the children, a rental house for the fall when they'd have to leave the rectory, and a job for the father. This also taught me something profound about courage—about willingness. Put yourself out there, listen to what's important to you, take a step, and amazing things happen.

By July I was interviewing with the outplacement firm my neighbor worked for. By September I had my first job as a career counselor. I went through training, shadowed other coaches, and then was given my first clients. It was a steep learning curve, but I loved it and felt I belonged. My colleagues were generous and helped me, and my neighbor (we often drove to work together) was a wonderful mentor.

I understand that some people might not see the connection between sponsoring a refugee family and starting a new career, but for me they're inseparable because I learned to listen to myself and didn't bully myself into doing work I knew I didn't want to do. Through the process of working with the refugee family, I gained the confidence to do things I hadn't done before. It was, in the true sense of the expression, a win-win.

Sixteen years later the two girls have graduated from college and one is married and just gave birth to her first child (whom I jokingly call "made in America"). The parents both have good jobs and they own their own home. Over the years, they've helped other families resettle in our area. In fact, there are so many Bosnian families now, that when they get together (and these are people who know how to party), they have to use the community center because there are too many to fit in anyone's home. And I'm still doing work I love, now with my third outplacement firm. How bad is that?

Quick Do's and Don'ts

Do:

1. Use this involuntary break from work to explore things that call to you.

2. Connect with your community in activities that you enjoy, whether it be sports, the arts, crafts, or a social cause.

3. Be as creative as you can in organizing what you're doing. Variety keeps things interesting.

Don't:

1. Get stuck in front of your computer all day. This is not productive and will not make you feel very good.

2. Assume that you know how you're going to find your next job.

3. Let panic force you to limit your interaction with others. Most of us need a little push to get out the door and try new things. I believe you'll find, as I did, that new opportunities come from connections.

Resources and Ideas

So here we are at the end of this journey, having looked at the shock of job loss and how to get past it, having explored myths that get in the way of running a productive search, and having examined the way forward. You've met a lot of people—many with inspiring stories and some who got stuck. My hope through all of this is that it has been helpful—that you realize now that you have company and that these new friends you've met in these pages accompany you on this critical mission: finding your next job.

- If you've been keeping a journal and you look back to your first few days of job loss, you'll see that you have changed. It may still bother you to be in transition, but you hopefully understand that this happens to many people and that you have to move on.

- You know what you need to do to find a new opportunity. You know what you need to support your search. And through the stories I've shared with you—all true stories of real clients who have lost their jobs and looked for new ones—I hope you've seen how surprising and diverse this process is.

- As promised at the beginning of this book, you have to go through this only once. Only once will you be unprepared for job loss, only once will you be stunned and not know what to do. But now, as you've learned from the many others who have gone through this and have found new jobs, you have tools. You have specific examples that will help you find your way so that if you are downsized again, you'll be prepared and will know what to do.

- Your resume will be up to date and your network will be active.

- You'll be current in your function and industry. You might even have some ideas about what you'd like to do next. This is career resilience, and although many people might still wish for the old days where you worked for one company your entire working life, there is an advantage to being responsible for your own career. Managing your career is your job, no one else's. This allows you to make choices that are good for you. And my hope for you is that you find work you love—that engages you, allows you to make a difference, and keeps you learning. It doesn't get any better than that.

CHAPTER 41

IN HIS OWN WORDS:
THE TRUTH OR NOT

While searching for a job, I found that everyone knows the gospel truth about how to go about finding a job. It worked for them and is therefore absolutely the best and only way to go about a job search. The advice ran the gamut, from "plaster the Internet with searches and apply for every job that comes up" to "send personal letters to every CFO in your industry and follow up with a phone call to introduce yourself."

The thing I learned was that none of the advice was wrong, but each piece of advice could be disastrous if implemented in a vacuum. Every piece of advice and guidance I received while in my job transition contained at least a grain of truth and had value if taken in the context of a larger job search plan. Thanks to really good guidance from a small number of friends and colleagues, I figured out after a time that there is no magic bullet in job search. So I went about my search doing my best to discount the half-truths and avoid the obstacles.

My story, with all its twists and turns and ups and downs, is a success story. I had a new position exactly five months from my first day of unemployment, I met some really great (and a few not so great) people, and I am certainly much better prepared if unemployment ever comes my way again.

My Story

Looking back, I can see that I was lucky in so many ways, but it didn't feel that way when I found out in February 2008 that I was losing my job. I really had it good; I was a senior finance and accounting professional at a major publisher of children's books in New York City. I was well liked and respected all the way up the food chain. I made a very comfortable living. But I had never been unemployed before and I hadn't seen this one coming. I didn't even have an updated resume. My Rolodex was out of date and the company didn't want me to tell anyone internally for what turned out to be two months as they prepared an announcement. So I ended up living a lie at the office during that time—quite a way to start looking for a new job.

A day or two after I was notified of my job loss, I made my first good decision: I swallowed my pride, picked up the phone, and reached out to ask for help. I called two former colleagues who had been through this before and asked them what to do. I was admittedly more focused on getting help with how to handle my severance package, but as a result of putting myself out there I was able to realize early on that people were not judgmental and did want to help if they could.

Unfortunately, though, I spent the first two months doing pretty much nothing that got me closer to a new position. I negotiated a very fair package that included severance, some health benefits, and outplacement services. I updated my resume, had some lunches, and spoke to some recruiters, all the regular stuff. However, I was still working and was in the office five days a week. I didn't have the "time," or more honestly the motivation, to do what I would come to realize it took to find my next job. This ongoing work continued until mid-August. Yes, I kept working for six months after I found out I was let go. By the time I was officially unemployed, it was August 2008—the month before Lehman Brothers failed and all hell broke loose in our economy. So I, and millions of others in the U.S., started collecting unemployment compensation in September 2008.

But from about mid-April until the end of August was my fat, dumb, and happy time. I was working Tuesday through Friday, and on Mondays I would attend outplacement near home. At outplacement I joined a "networking team" of other unemployed people who got together weekly to discuss successes, failures, strategies, and opportunities. This was really where I started to get my first view into what running a job search was about and the effort and commitment it would take to find my next opportunity. Unlike me, my teammates were living on their severance and unemployment compensation, sometimes just unemployment compensation. The successful ones, defined as those who found jobs, came to team meetings talking about how many new contacts they spoke to that week by phone and in person and how each one might help them in one way or another. This was really my first clue that networking tended to be more effective than other methods of job search.

It took me a month or so to figure this out, and during that time I did all the easy stuff: updated my resume, posted it online, and set up job searches online. During this time I also put together what the outplacement company called a marketing plan. It included a professional summary, a list of my skill sets and expertise, and an outline of my target market, including company size and location, and specific organizations I was interested in working for. I called it my profile and it quickly became my networking bible.

Armed with a resume and profile, I was ready to get to the real work: networking. I started to set networking goals for myself in midsummer. Because I was still working part time, I started slowly, meeting with three people a week to get job leads and additional contacts. That's how it works; you can't just get network contacts from the phone book, so you have to impress people enough when you meet them that they are willing to introduce you to their friends and colleagues. I started by making a list of people I already knew. To my great surprise, I had almost 50 people to start with.

The toughest call to make is the first one, so I chickened out and sent an e-mail instead. But to my shock, the person called me the next day and we had coffee the next week. I continued along this path for the rest of the summer and into the fall with a few interviews mixed in. The really interesting part about taking this approach to job search was that even though I had not landed in a new position yet, I didn't feel like a failure. To the contrary, I was meeting people and expanding my network by leaps and bounds.

Once I met people face to face, they were really interested in helping however they could. Most gave me contacts to network with, some introduced me to networking groups that they belonged to, and many introduced me to their recruiters. I met people for breakfast, lunch, dinner, coffee, drinks, or just in their office, and I went wherever was most convenient for them. I found that Starbucks was always convenient to people's offices, so I drank a lot of coffee.

I had only a few rules about these meetings: I always paid, I never asked for a job, and I always asked whether they could help me expand my network. In my experience, meeting in person was a key to success. The phone was too impersonal, which made it easier for them to not help, and electronic means such as e-mail, LinkedIn, Facebook, and so on were easily and often ignored.

Before I knew it, it was September 30. Summer was over and I had been out of work for over a month. I continued to keep very busy meeting new people, attending networking group meetings, applying for job postings, speaking to recruiters, going to my kids' sports events, having lunch with my wife, cleaning up my garden, getting in shape, and catching up on my reading. Job search for me was not a 40-hour-a-week endeavor, and the stress of being unemployed was somewhat offset by the satisfaction I got out of my successful networking and the pure enjoyment of spending more time with my family.

The month of October was more of the same. I had the odd interview and a second interview thrown in, which was good because it helped me practice my interview skills and stay positive and focused. Then it happened: The last week in October I was attending a state conference for school board members. But before I went, I sent out a flurry of e-mails to set up appointments, follow up on contacts, and touch base with people that I hadn't spoken to for the past six weeks. A couple of days later I was on the convention floor and my phone rang. It was not a number I recognized and I could barely hear because of the noise level, but in job search mode I always picked up. It was an old colleague to whom I had sent a simple five-line catch-up e-mail that week. We exchanged pleasantries and I apologized for the noise level. Then he said, "I think I have the perfect job for you."

Turns out that this network contact was doing some consulting for a company in my industry that was looking for a new CFO. Two and a half months later, after a number of interviews and a couple of weeks of compensation negotiation, I was sitting in my new office as the new CFO of a small privately held educational publishing company.

My Truth

My truth is that you never know where the next opportunity will come from, and the best practice is to leave no stone unturned. My new job happened to come from a single e-mail that basically said, "How are you doing? Let's get together for coffee soon." I often wonder what I would be doing now if I hadn't sent that e-mail. Odds are that I would not have known about the opportunity without it.

But I don't just chalk it up to luck or fate; if I hadn't conducted a complete job search with multiple elements, I would have been short-changing no one but myself. A new job could have easily come through a recruiter or an Internet submission, and I got interviews through these channels as well. In the end it was networking that worked for me. It required the most work, but in my specific search it produced the desired result. I am hopeful that maintaining my core network will also serve me over the long term. As someone said to me in my search, "Jobs are temporary; job search is permanent."

Kennedy D. Paul
CFO, Bill Smith Group

APPENDIX A

JOB SEARCH SCHEDULES

Daily:

8:00–9:30: Check e-mail, major job boards, and top company Web sites.

9:30–11:00: Review your networking spreadsheet to see who needs a follow-up call or e-mail, and reach out to five new contacts.

11:00–11:30: Break time. Walk the dog, run on the treadmill, have a snack.

11:30–12:30: Research top companies and write a draft of a tailored target letter (see appendix B).

12:30–1:30: Break for lunch and errands.

1:30–3:00: Research professional associations, industry groups, or job search support meetings and sign up to attend their meetings.

> **Note:** If you need to end your day here, include some of the networking mentioned in the 3–5 p.m. time slot. You've put in five and a half hours of work, which is enough to produce good results if you maintain this five days a week.

3:00–5:00: Review your networking contacts (including LinkedIn) to see whether you can find a contact at your top companies. Think about what you've accomplished and prioritize what you must do tomorrow. Write this down so that it's the first thing you see when you report to your desk the next day.

Weekly:

Monday: Review Internet postings and research top companies.

Tuesday: Review your networking spreadsheet, add new contacts, and reach out to at least 10 people (by e-mail or phone).

Wednesday: Contact recruiters, whether through referrals (important for retained recruiters) or from a list (Kennedy Information's *Directory of Executive & Professional Recruiters* or online resources), and get your resume out to at least 15.

Thursday: Research professional associations and try to find meetings in your area. If you can't, see whether you can obtain association directories. These are a wonderful source of people in your function or industry. Follow up on Tuesday's networking calls.

Friday: Review your week, see what needs more time and attention, and pick a few companies to target directly.

Monthly:

Here are suggestions for organizing your search on a month-by-month basis. Because it's difficult to predict how long your search will take, you may follow these steps in any time frame.

- Get your documents and verbal communications in order.
- Create your search map and implementation timeline.
- Make sure networking is your major activity and practice your verbal communications.
- Prepare for interviews and try to schedule networking meetings with people you don't know. This is a great way to practice for interviews.
- Review progress and see whether it's time to create and implement a plan B. Make sure you're taking advantage of professional associations and job search meetings.
- Make sure your follow-up is timely and effective. Circle back to people you haven't spoken with in a while.
- Reach out to more recruiters and refresh your resume on all postings.
- Ask a few people to review your search goals, strategy, and execution. Make changes as needed to create more activity.
- Consider contract work or consulting as a way to get back to work and open new doors. Register with agencies that specialize in this.
- Implement plan B. It's time to bring in income.
- Send out e-mail blasts so that your network is up to date and knows you're still looking while you engage in temporary work.
- Thank those who have been most helpful over the past year and reach out to new contacts through professional associations or volunteering.

THE TARGET E-MAIL

Use this format to interest companies that have not advertised a position and when you are not working with a recruiter. If you have a contact, just add a first line stating, "[contact's name] recommended that I write you." Send this type of e-mail to the person who would hire you—the decision maker—not human resources (unless you seek a job in HR, of course). Consider sending the e-mail without a resume so that you come across as a problem solver rather than a job seeker, and thus are not directed away from the hiring manager. (Also, an e-mail without an attachment is more likely to be read.)

Research is critical for maximum impact. If you've identified 10 companies of interest to you, research at least 4 or 5. Obtain the latest financial and product information and use it in your first sentence. For example, you might write

As an emerging biotech firm with three new products to prepare for FDA approval, you need a chemist with extensive analytical and laboratory experience.

In other words, link what they need with what you have to offer. Then prove you can help them by following the rest of the following format.

Dear _____:

*(This **must** be a person's name, spelled correctly, not a "Dear Sir or Madam or Hiring Manager.")*

(Pick one of these two beginnings)

If you need a _____ with expertise in _____ and _____, we should talk.

(Or)

As a _____ with more than _____ years of expertise in _____, I know that I could be a profitable addition to your company.

(Prove It!)

For example, in my position as _____ at a large _____ firm, I:

(List three accomplishments)

> Increased…
> Initiated…
> Developed…

(Personalize your accomplishments)

What I'm really good at is _____. I know the _____ market and how to _____. (You can add another example/accomplishment here if needed.) I'm certain I could do the same for your company.

I'll call you next week to arrange a mutually convenient time for us to talk.

Sincerely,

(Your name, e-mail, and phone number)

Figure B.1: Target e-mail template.

APPENDIX C

SEARCH MAPS

A search map serves two major purposes: as a guide or compass to you in your search and as a key networking tool. There are many different ways to set up a search map, but here's a sample template. Many job seekers have found this a more effective tool than a resume for getting help from others.

Titles or Objectives:
Administrative Assistant
Receptionist
Customer Service Support

Key Skills or Competencies:
Microsoft Office
Written and verbal communications
Handling multiple tasks simultaneously
Confidentiality

The Market:
Location—Central Florida in the Orlando region
Industries—Educational institutions, nonprofits, and government
Size—Open
Culture—Fast paced, growing

Target Companies:
(This is where you put your list of 30 to 50 companies that might be of interest to you. Do not base this list on job openings, but simply use the market definitions that you've created above to determine your list. If you have several types of organizations, list the companies under headings like the following.)

Educational	**Nonprofits**	**Government**

Figure C.1: Sample search map 1.

Titles or Objectives:
Director of Marketing
Senior Marketing Manager

Key Skills or Competencies:
     Marketing strategy
     Online marketing
     Communications
     Team management
     Advertising
     Market research
     Public relations
     Event management

The Market:
Chicago area
Oregon coast (second choice)

Target Companies:
(Here you create your list of 30 to 50 companies. In this case, you could organize them by location.)

Chicago area   **Oregon coast**

Figure C.2: Sample search map 2.

APPENDIX D

PLAN B

Generally I advise clients to put their plan B in motion if they have not found a job within 10 months. Depending on your finances, you may want to implement this sooner. Here are additional ways to bring in income:

- Consulting
- Contract work
- Go back to work with your previous company (this happens more often than you'd expect)
- Unrelated work that is easier to get: delivering newspapers, driving a limousine, landscaping, retail jobs, and so on
- Work that is beyond the geography set out in your search map (see appendix C)
- Work that is a lower level than your most recent employment (for example, if you're in finance and you could decide to work for H & R Block during tax time)
- Helping a friend who runs her or his own business

Additional note on plan Bs: What many of the clients I've worked with have done is to take something that gives them both income and structure but that doesn't interfere with their job search efforts. For example, one of my marketing clients took an evening and weekend job in retail. As she put it, "Working at the cosmetics counter gave me a great employee discount and lots of free high-end products, which made me feel better during my search." And of course it also helped her meet her expenses.

BUSINESS CARD EXAMPLES

Here is a business card format you can follow:

Name

Generic Title

Three bullets that highlight key skills or industries

E-mail address

Phone number

LinkedIn URL

Here are some examples of business cards created using this format:

Jane Smith
Senior Marketing Director

- Financial Services
- IT
- Publishing

Jane.Smith@me.com
Cell: (609) 896-4567
www.linkedin.com/in/janesmith

Joseph Christopher
Data-Entry Clerk

- Excellent keyboard skills
- Known for multitasking
- Attention to detail

Joseph.Christopher@fantastic.com
Home: (732) 555-3456
www.linkedin.com/in/josephchristopher

You can create your own business card from your computer if you buy business card stock. Or you can order free cards from VistaPrint (www.vistaprint.com). VistaPrint has a wide variety of colors and designs.

Also, to set up your personal URL on LinkedIn, go to frequently asked questions on www.linkedin.com and follow the directions.

THE INTERVIEW MAP

The purpose of an interview map is to prepare you to "manage" the interview, or at least to include critical parts of your background in the interview process and to help you keep track of what you've covered with each interviewer.

To develop an interview map, put the name of the company and the interviewer's name and title at the top of the page. Make one of these sheets for every person you're meeting with. Draw a two-column table. On the left side, list key components of the job, as you know it from your research. On the right side, put keywords to remind you of your accomplishments or credentials.

Research is critical in preparing an effective interview map, and you might also need to ask questions during the interview to make sure that the information you found is accurate and relevant.

ABC Company
Interview with John D. Smith, CFO, for Controller position

Key Components of Position	My Matching Accomplishments
Administrative protocols	Written manuals, changed payroll week
Changes in staffing and job functions	Fiscal unit development and changes
Daily operations	Fiscal unit, supervise 10 FTE, volunteers
Utilizing volunteers, work-study students	Started as a volunteer liaison
Annual appraisals, salary increases	Done it for 16 years
Financial accounting & bookkeeping	6 years in accounting
A/R, A/P, purchasing	Did it with support & directly (rent)
GL, adjusting entries	Monthly routine with A/R, cash flow, and A/P
Operational & Capital budgets	Budget Coordinator, Fiscal Unit
Monthly financials	Routine, February did all, including investments, cash flow, long-term debt
Audits	Routine program and finance
Purchasing with directors and university	Fiscal support unit, purchasing coordinator
Government contracts, outside consultants	IS project, $12M in government contracts
Computer resources and database	IS project, written databases
Communications with other divisions	Liaison within GNY & NHQ
Special events	Volunteer recognition, auction
Long- and short-term plans for capital improvements	Budget coordinator, fiscal unit, purchasing
Office space	Logistics (TWA)

1. What is the greatest challenge facing the person in this position?
2. Are there any areas where I haven't given you enough information?
3. Would the Controller have any direct reports?

Figure F.1: Sample interview map.

Notice that I added three prepared questions at the bottom of the map. You may not need these, but it's helpful to have prepared questions before the interview.

You can take notes on your map, checking off as key areas are covered. This is particularly helpful in all-day interviews.

IMPLEMENTATION TIMELINE

You might find it easier to add this implementation timeline to your job search schedule (see appendix A), especially if you create a monthly schedule. The most important factor is to have a clear sense of your financial needs—which is what determines your timeline.

- Sit down with a financial planner so that you know what to do with your 401K and have a solid sense of how long you can last without using your savings.

- In months 1 to 3, use your severance and bank your unemployment check in case your search goes longer than expected.

- When severance runs out, cut expenses so that your unemployment compensation will go further.

- Make sure you have your plan B in place so that you know how you might earn some additional income (see appendix D) well before you need it.

- Analyze what has been effective so far in your search and adjust your daily efforts so that you're doing more of the things that are getting results.

- Seek outside advice from a career counselor, a recruiter you know well, or friends who have been through this process recently. Share your schedule and goals and see whether they have ideas to help make your search more productive.

- Pay attention to what keeps you motivated and effective in this challenging work. A great example of this is Ken Paul's story in chapter 41.

- Enlist your family's help so that running your search and managing your finances aren't solely on your shoulders. One of my clients had to dramatically reduce her teenage daughter's shopping budget. But once her daughter understood why this was important, she found other ways to save money.

- Prepare for any obstacles that you can anticipate, and seek outside help. For example, if you have a child in college, make sure to tell the financial aid office that you've lost your job so that you can take advantage of additional resources.

APPENDIX H

SUGGESTED READING

Bolles, Richard Nelson. *What Color Is Your Parachute? A Practical Manual for Job-Hunters and Career-Changers.* Berkeley: Ten Speed Press, 2010.

Cameron, Julia. *The Artist's Way: A Spiritual Path to Higher Creativity.* New York: Tarcher/Perigee Books, 1992.

Farr, Michael, and Gaither, Dick. *Next-Day Job Interview.* Indianapolis: JIST Publishing, 2009.

Fox, Jeffrey J. *How to Land Your Dream Job: No Resume! And Other Secrets to Get You in the Door.* New York: Hyperion, 2006.

Jeffers, Susan. *Feel the Fear and Do It Anyway.* New York: Reed Business Information Inc., 1987, and reprinted by Ballantine Books, 2006.

The Directory of Executive Recruiters. Peterborough, NH: Kennedy Information Publishers, published annually since 1971.

Pierson, Orville. *The Unwritten Rules of the Highly Effective Job Search.* New York: McGraw-Hill, 2006.

Pierson, Orville. *Highly Effective Networking—Meet the Right People and Get a Great Job.* Franklin Lakes, NJ: Career Press, 2009.

Piotrowski, Katy. *The Career Coward's Guide to Interviewing.* Indianapolis: JIST Publishing, 2007.

Reed Aboud, Sharon. *All Moms Work: Short-term Strategies for Long-range Success.* Herndon, VA: Capital Books, 2009.

Ryan, Robin. *Sixty Seconds and You're Hired!* New York: Penguin, 2009.

Tieger, Paul and Barbara Barron. *Do What You Are: Discover the Perfect Career for You Through the Secrets of Personality Type.* New York: Little, Brown and Company, 1992.

Whitcomb, Susan Britton. *Interview Magic: Job Interview Secrets from America's Career and Life Coach.* Indianapolis: JIST Publishing, 2008.

Yate, Martin. *Knock 'Em Dead—The Ultimate Job Search Guide 2010.* Avon, MA: Adams Media, 2010.

INDEX

About the Author

Jean Baur is a Senior Consultant with the nation's leading outplacement firm, Lee Hecht Harrison, which has 240 offices worldwide. She has partnered with thousands of clients to help them overcome job loss and recession-proof their careers. In addition, she designs and delivers workshops to improve clients' interviewing and overall search skills.

Jean's trademark is her humor and creativity. She loves nothing better than brainstorming with a client to transform an unproductive search into a successful one. She is a writer with extensive freelance credits, including work for Educational Testing Service. She has also trained more than 10,000 middle and senior managers in presentation skills and business writing.

Notes

Notes

Notes

Notes

Notes

Notes

Notes